K
3215
£3.25

This picture: The first example of the new Sea Harrier version of the British Aerospace 'Jump Jet' made its maiden flight in August 1978 and is seen here over the BAe Aircraft Group, Kingston-Brough Division airfield at Dunsfold, Surrey. / *British Aerospace*

aircraft ILLUSTRATED annual

1980

Edited by Martin Horseman

LONDON
IAN ALLAN LTD

Contents

This picture: One of the many Harvard trainers preserved in airworthy condition in the UK is this camouflaged Mk IIB, G-AZSC, formerly FT 323 in RAF service and also operated later by the RNethAF. / *Gordon Bain*

First published 1979

ISBN 0 7110 0936 8

Published by Ian Allan Ltd, Shepperton, Surrey; and printed in the United Kingdom by Ian Allan Printing Ltd

The BAe146

British Aerospace's first aircraft

PHILIP BIRTLES

Above: A full scale wooden mock-up of the BAe 146 at Hatfield; complete with fully furnished cabin and detailed cockpit layout, the replica of the airliner is used for demonstrations to prospective customers. / *BAe Hatfield*

After nearly four years on the stocks, the British Aerospace BAe146 feeder-liner, formerly known as the Hawker Siddeley HS146, was relaunched in mid-1978. Originally announced on 29 August 1973 as a joint project with the Government sharing 50% of the £120m development costs and Hawker Siddeley the other 50% plus any over-runs, the HS146 appeared as a high wing, four fan-jet-powered feeder-liner with a range of up to 1,500 nautical miles, but optimised for multi-stop operations with stage lengths of around 150nm. However, the advent of the unexpected and so-called 'fuel crisis' in 1974, had an adverse effect on the project's operational prospects, and the HS146 appeared to have been given the go-ahead at an unfortunate time. Not only did fuel become vastly more expensive overnight, but the world economies took a knock with the sudden galloping inflation. Hawker Siddeley could see little prospect of quoting a reasonable price for the aircraft which the airlines could afford and which would make a fair profit to the company. A price quoted on one day could well be making a ridiculous loss a month later. The airlines themselves were not faring much better and the general feeling was to soldier on with existing equipment until the situation became more stable.

Hawker Siddeley Aviation therefore recommended to the Government that work should stop on the project, since if it continued the cost over-runs would in effect be more than the combined resources of the Hawker Siddeley Group could absorb, resulting in a likely financial collapse of the entire Group. Either the Government would have had to bail out the company or all the money would have been lost to no avail, causing widespread loss of jobs throughout many areas of industry. Work therefore stopped on the HS146 at 16.00hrs on 21 October 1974 after growing rumours of its demise at the previous Farnborough Show.

BAe146 series 100 and 200

	Srs 100	Srs 200
Engines (both)	Four Avco Lycoming ALF 502H turbofans (length: 56.8in (1.44m); weight: 1,245lb (565kg)) developing 6,700lb (3,039kg) static thrust with by pass ratio of 5.9:1	
Span (both)	86ft 6in (26.36m)	
Length	85ft 10in (26.16m)	93ft 1in (28.38m)
Height (both)	28ft 3in (8.61m)	
Wing Area (both)	832ft^2 (77.3m^2)	
Cabin Internal Width (both)	11ft 1in (3.48m)	
Underfloor Cargo Volume	500ft^3 (14.16m^3)	674ft^3 (19.10m^3)
Design Speed Vmo/Mmo	315kt CAS/0.7Mach	300kt CAS/0.7Mach
Max Take-off Weight	73,850lb (33,500kg)	87,500lb (39,700kg)
Max Landing Weight	71,850lb (32,590kg)	77,000lb (34,930kg)
Max Zero Fuel Weight	61,250lb (27,780kg)	68,500lb (31,070kg)
Operating Empty Weight	43,000lb (19,500kg)	46,000lb (20,900kg)
Standard Fuel Capacity (both)	2,540 Imp gal (3,050 US gal, 11,546 litre)	
Optional Fuel Capacity (both)	2,840 Imp gal (3,410 US gal, 12,911 litre)	
Seating Capacity	70-90 passengers	80-109 passengers

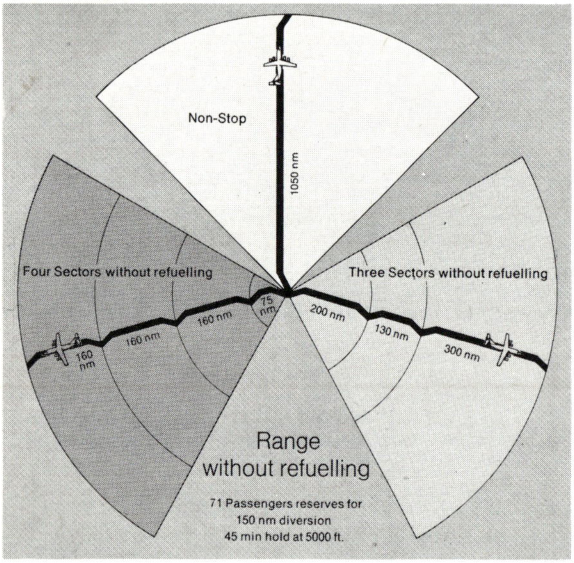

Above: A diagram showing the planned performance of the BAe146 over a range of short-haul sectors; the aircraft's high design landing weight and low fuel consumption will permit quick turn-rounds on multi-stop operations without the need for intermediate refuelling. / *BAe*

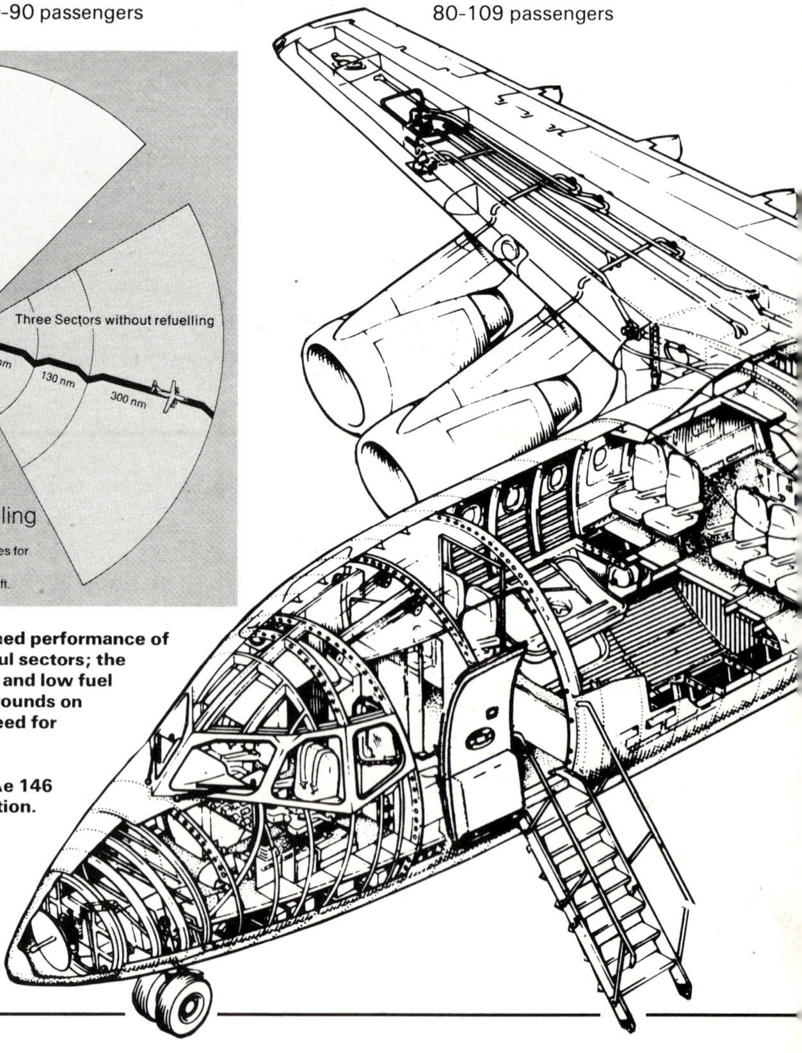

Right: Cutaway drawing showing BAe 146 structure, systems, and accommodation. / *BAe*

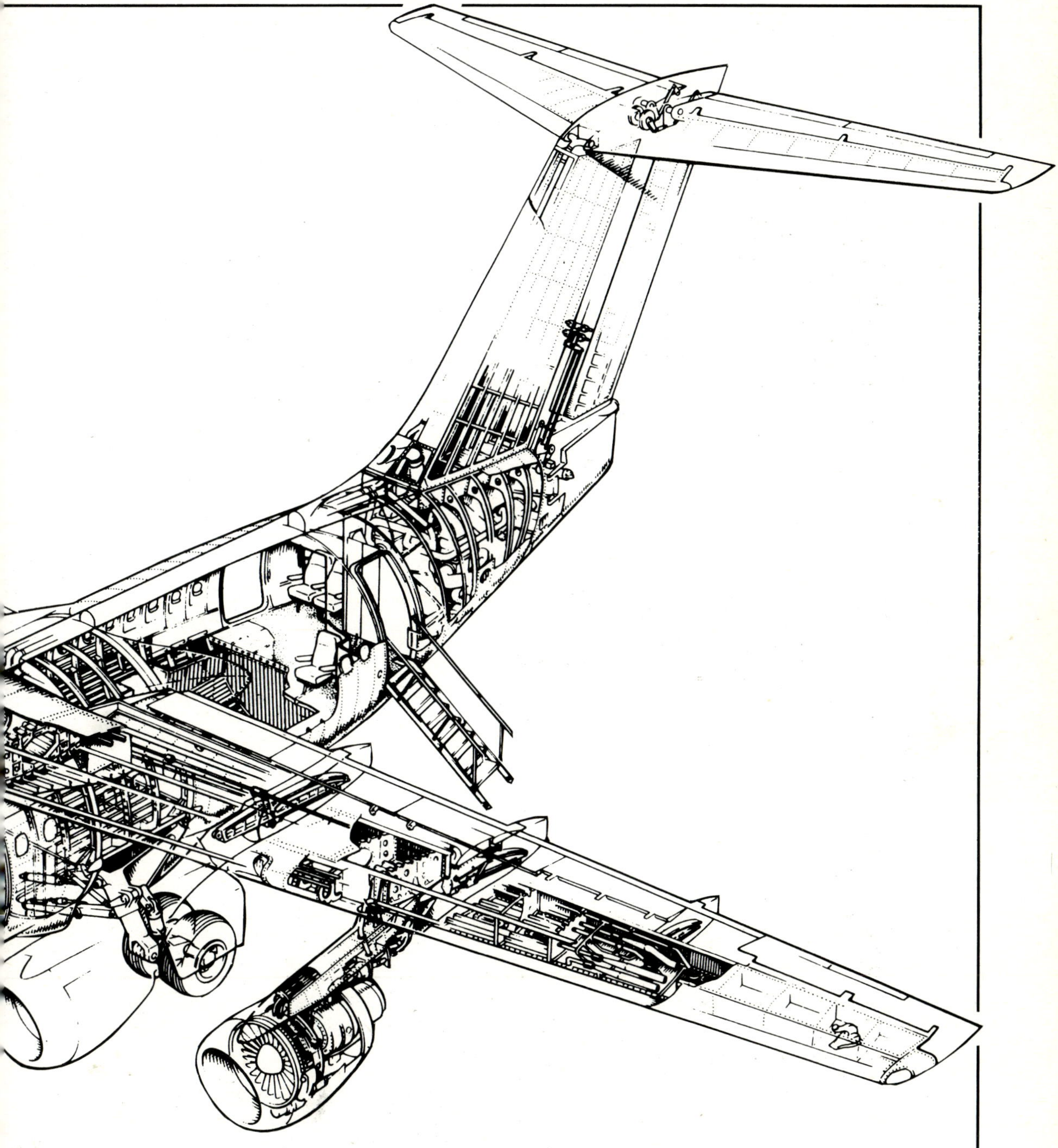

Above: Artist's impression of the 'new' airliner — a view dating, in fact, from the time when it was the HS146, but showing well the aircraft's high wing, and four engine configuration. / *Photo via the Author*

Fortunately the project was not allowed to die. Protest marches were organised by the unions and much hard lobbying was done with members of parliament, particularly Helene Hayman, Labour member for the marginal Welwyn/Hatfield seat. As a result the Government sanctioned relatively small sums of money for the project to be kept alive by allowing design refinement of the structure and systems, some structural testing of test pieces and eventually, as the money became available, the completion of a set of main assembly jigs for the manufacture of the major airframe test specimens.

Meanwhile Hawker Siddeley Aviation, the British Aircraft Corporation and Scottish Aviation were merged as the nationalised British Aerospace (BAe), the airframe manufacturing components of the private sector companies being welded into the new BAe Aircraft Group. Early BAe evaluation of the civil air transport market underlined that the airline industry was becoming more stable and in need of new equipment. Although the Fokker F28 had been under development and in production for about 15 years, it was felt that its development potential was restricted and that there was obvious room for improvement using the latest techniques in structural simplicity, ease of maintenance, reliability, economy and quietness of operation. The market still stood at about 1,200 aircraft required in the 70-100-seat feeder-liner class, of which British Aerospace conservatively expected to sell 360 BAe146s, leaving plenty of room for a good competitor.

During 1977 BAe Aircraft Group Hatfield-Chester Division at Hatfield could see a good case emerging for restarting the project and eventually convinced the British Aerospace main board. This resulted in the Chairman, Lord Beswick, writing to the Government on 22 March 1978 recommending that the BAe146 be relaunched and seeking formal approval. A number of MPs were briefed on the aircraft and approval was given for a relaunch, with little prior warning, in Parliament on Monday afternoon, 10 July 1978.

At a hastily convened press conference at Hatfield next day, British Aerospace presented the details of the aircraft. Following studies with 162 airlines world wide, it had been established that average stage distances for existing feeder operations was 151 statute miles, the BAe146 being aimed initially as a replacement for the many prop-jet aircraft still flying but coming up for retirement in the next decade. In addition 63 airlines had an average small twin-jet operation of 305 statute miles.

As before, the BAe146 would be powered by four Avco Lycoming ALF 502-H fan-jet engines developing 6,700lb thrust each, based on a core engine with over three million hr experience. Although the Rolls-Royce M45 powerplant had been considered, it could not match the American engine on first cost or operational costs, but it could easily be adopted by an operator at a later date. However, the airlines need to operate at a profit and four ALF 502s with their straightforward 'on condition', modular maintenance, excellent take-off performance and en-route economy, provided by far the best answer. They also give a quiet operation for use in down-town airports, the 90 PNdB footprint covering 2.2sq miles as compared with 4.2sq miles with a typical twin turboprop and 7.5sq miles for a twin-jet. The new aircraft will easily comply with all current and known noise legislation throughout the

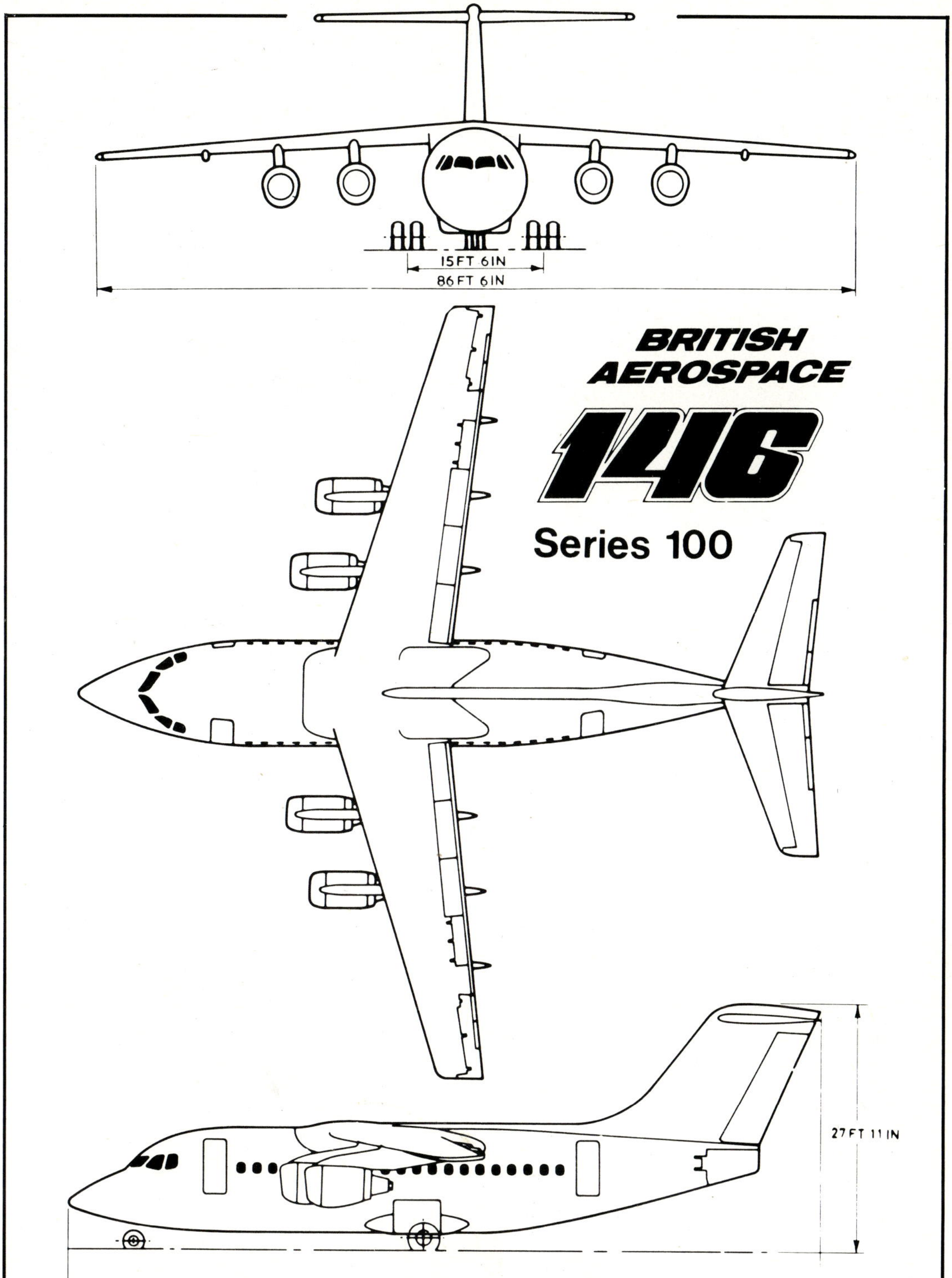
15 FT 6 IN
86 FT 6 IN
BRITISH AEROSPACE
146
Series 100
27 FT 11 IN
85 FT 10 IN

Above: The interior of the BAe 146 mock-up at Hatfield shows the roominess of the passenger cabin with its five-abreast seat layout. / *BAe Hatfield*

world and will be able to operate from runways less than 3,500ft in length, with exceptional performance capabilities from high altitude, high temperature airfields. Take-offs and landings will be possible from both unpaved and low bearing-strength runways; the aircraft's sideways-retracting, fuselage-mounted main undercarriage having a wider track than that of the Lockheed C-130 Hercules.

For maximum comfort, the cabin of the projected BAe146-100 initial model of the aircraft will have a shoulder height width of 128in (325cm) and five-abreast seating at a 33in pitch, giving room for 71 passengers in addition to the two flight crew. Alternatively, with six-abreast seating and a 31in pitch, 88 passengers can be carried. The longer, series 200 version of the BAe 146 will carry from 80-109 passengers, and both versions will have a small galley at the front and a toilet at either end. If a 96in by 75in cargo door is fitted on the port side at the front end of the cabin, two 108in by 88in pallets could be carried at the front end plus 39 passengers five-abreast at a 31in pitch. Adequate emergency exits are provided for with the normal entrances, the passengers entering through the rear door in the mixed passenger/freight layout. For all-freight operation four 108in by 88in pallets plus one 108in by 60in pallet can be carried. The underfloor baggage compartments have centrally placed doors for easy access to netted-off compartments for each destination on a multi-stop operation, and there is adequate room for any engine modules or spare main wheel in the event of an aircraft going unservicable at a remote out-station.

In addition to the civil versions there is a considerable military potential for this type of aircraft. An analysis was made of medium rear-loading military transports operating in countries with a fleet of five or more aircraft, excluding USA, USSR, Eastern Europe and China, and approximately 790 are in operation. In addition there are approximately 1,335 non-rear-loading turboprop and piston engined types operating under a similar coverage. By adapting the BAe146 to a rear-loading tactical transport by lowering the floor level, British Aerospace estimate that they can achieve at least 100 sales in this important market. As well as lowering the floor level and modifying the rear fuselage for a loading ramp, the main undercarriage units would be located in fuselage fairings to give the internal clearance. Typical loads for the military '146', would be a Scorpion tank weighing 17,500lb and a half-ton truck, or a one-ton truck, a 105mm light gun and a half-ton truck.

The aircraft is to be built in production modules already partly equipped prior to assembly, so any centre fuselage or rear fuselage modifications can be easily fed into the production line.

The design, development, manufacture of the nose and flight deck, final assembly, flight testing, sales and product support will all be located at Hatfield. The centre fuselage section, with the wing centre section and main undercarriage pick - up, will be a BAe Aircraft Group Weybridge-Bristol Division

Left: The BAe 146 cockpit canopy assembly jig shown practically complete and ready to accept components.

Below: The airliner's fuselage centre section assembly jig being completed at Hatfield in early-1978 for the assembly of structural test specimens.
/ *BAe Hatfield*

Above: This artist's impression of the new airliner in service shows how it will be capable of transforming the scale and economics of air travel possibilities to remote locations.

Right: A half model of the BAe 146 on the floor of the low speed wind tunnel at Hatfield for airflow tests — note the rows of tufts positioned on the fuselage, wing and engine pods.
/ BAe Hatfield

responsibility at Filton and the rear fuselage will be built by the Manchester Division. SAAB are producing parts on a risk sharing basis, and Avco are to build the wing on the same basis. The wing was previously to be produced by Aerospatiale at Nantes, but only as a sub-contractor as they had no wish to share in the risks. Although there was a great outcry in the press about 40% of the work possibly going overseas on a risk sharing basis, it will in effect enlarge the 'home market' resulting in more sales prospects and therefore more work for British Aerospace.

Avco Lycoming will still supply the engines as a normal contractor, but the wings may be built by their Aerostructures Div which has already produced wings for the Gulfstream II, C-141 Starlifter and the giant C-5A Galaxy. An example of how useful a significant North American content can be is provided by the HS125 business jet, which is equipped, furnished, and painted in North America for that market where over 200 sales have resulted — more than 50% of the world total.

It has been estimated that the project will cost £250m to launch, and bring 7,000 jobs within British Aerospace, in the majority of cases safeguarding existing jobs, and creating 4,000-5,000 with the suppliers of equipment. As the programme builds up, other British Aerospace factories with production capacity could also be involved in the programme, but this aircraft is only part of the overall civil aircraft strategy of the company which includes programme participation on variants of the Airbus A300 and a 160 to 180-seater airliner known as JET2 (a second series Joint European Transport).

Above: The BAe 146 will operate out of short airfields, regardless of unpaved or low bearing strength runways. With a payload of 71 passengers and baggage, the series 100 will have a range of over 1,000nm with full reserves; options are available for stage lengths as long as 1,400nm with the same payload. / *BAe Hatfield*

With work already started in the jigs at Hatfield on the structural test specimens, and some parts of the first aircraft already in store, the programme is ready to move into top gear, with the maiden flight of the BAe 146-100 scheduled for November 1980. The Certificate of Airworthiness is expected in early 1982 for first deliveries soon after, with the series 200 not far behind. The development of the military version will follow the series 200 and before the mid-1980s the Hatfield production line will be building three BAe146s a month for airlines and air forces in all the continents of the world. Now that the aircraft has been launched, almost too late, the selling has started and it is hoped that the first customers will have been announced by mid 1979.

25 Years of Lightnings

ROGER LINDSAY

Above: 'Sheer performance' ... a Lightning F3 of 2T Squadron streaks across the airfield at RAF Finningley during a solo display in September 1973. / *Martin Horseman*

Right: A Lightning T5, XS457 of No 2T Squadron from RAF Coltishall nears the top of a climbing turn while heading back towards the Norfolk coast. / *Richard Wilson*

The pastoral panorama of expansive East Anglian fields was verdant with thriving young crops and edged with clumps of Constable trees. It basked in the misty morning sunshine of early summer, and was relentlessly pushed downwards and behind us as we surged forward and headed for the North Sea, increasingly gathering momentum seconds after rotating from Wattisham's runway. Sheer exhilaration! ... sheer performance! ... such was our acceleration that even a deft movement of the stick occasioned by the need to make a slight course correction caused an immediate squeezing of the legs as my anti-G suit automatically responded to the induced force of 3G. Minutes later, and after exceeding 1,000mph on our way up, we levelled out at 60,000ft, where the sun blazed down through our Perspex canopy from out of a sky which was as dark as indigo velvet. The vehicle which had provided this thrill of a lifetime and transported me so close to Heaven was the greatest British fighter since the Spitfire — the Lightning.

Outstanding, unique — these two words seem to me the simplest and most appropriate to describe the remarkable Lightning, yet they are at the same time totally inadequate. The Lightning can streak skywards at over 50,000ft/min almost as soon as its pair of afterburning Rolls-Royce Avon engines have blasted it off the runway. The same engines can push it along effortlessly at 1,500mph on the level at altitude, and propel it to well over 15 miles high in a zoom climb. It's a pilot's aeroplane, responsive and tolerant, yet demanding enough to keep his adrenalin flowing for the full sortie. It is unique in design, in the arrangement of its engines, and in being the first RAF fighter planned from the outset as an integrated weapons system. More than anything, it is unique in being the only supersonic, Mach 2 aircraft of purely British design and manufacture ever to be produced in quantity. Aware of all these things it comes as something of a shock to realise that a quarter of a century has slipped by since I gazed at the first, coarse-screened photograph in the national newspapers, which signified the dêbut of the prototype aircraft in that first week of August 1954.

P

J

Above: The first air-to-air photograph to be released of the English Electric P1 research aircraft, WG760, the forerunner of the Lightning. / *English Electric Co Ltd*

Above left: A pair of camouflaged Lightnings seen at low level over the Humber. Nearer the camera is an F3, XR718, of No 5 Squadron, while beyond is an F6, XR752, of No 11 Squadron. / *Flt Lt T. R. Paxton RAF*

Below left: A Lightning F6 at high level — No 5 Squadron's 'J', XR725, showing the powerfully deep profile of the final production version to enter RAF service. / *Flt Lt T. R. Paxton RAF*

The photograph was heavily retouched so that neither the wing nor its tell-tale shadow should reveal its unique shape. At that time the aircraft was simply referred to as the English Electric P1, and the reason that the maiden flight of the first prototype, WG760, from Boscombe Down on 4 August 1954 attracted so much publicity was that here at last was tangible evidence of the aircraft billed to take the RAF into the realms of supersonic flight. That successful 30min first flight by English Electric's illustrious chief test pilot, Wg Cdr Roland 'Bee' Beamont, represented the tip of a technological iceberg which had originated back in 1947 when the then-Ministry of Supply issued Experimental Requirement 103 for a research aircraft capable of exploring transonic and low supersonic speeds of up to Mach 1.5. Fairey and English Electric submitted designs to ER 103, the former resulting in the FD2 record-breaking research aircraft, while the English Electric design, prosaically termed 'Project 1' (hence P1), had the built-in potential to be a combat aircraft. This was fortuitously timed, as it met many of the requirements of Air Ministry specification F23/49 for a supersonic day fighter. The genesis of the P1 design originated in the genius of W. E. W. Petter, although most of the subsequent development of that design became the responsibility of F. W. 'Freddie' Page who succeeded the legendary Teddy Petter as English Electric's chief design engineer after the latter migrated to Folland, where he went on to design the Midge and Gnat mini-fighters.

The initial P1 design featured wings swept sharply back at 60° and set low on the fuselage; the latter contained two axial-flow engines, fed from a simple nose air intake, arranged one above the other — originally the upper engine was ahead of the lower in contrast to the opposite layout which was adopted when the design was translated into metal. The tailplane, also swept at 60°, was originally low-set at the base of the fuselage to prevent transonic pitch-up. However, designers at RAE Farnborough remained sceptical on this score and argued that the tail should sit atop the fin, and this was actually put to the test on the specially constructed low-speed Short SB5. This aircraft flew in December 1952 and had wings similar in shape to those of the P1, which could be adjusted (on the ground) to settings of 50, 60, or 69° of sweep. Suffice it to say that, after 12 months of testing,

English Electric's 60° sweep wing and low-set tail were agreed as giving optimum results.

On 1 April 1950 two flight-test prototypes, WG760 and 763, had been ordered (together with a static-test airframe) and these were to be powered by two Armstrong-Siddeley Sapphire AS-Sa5 engines, offering 8,100lb dry thrust apiece, later supplemented by more than 2,000lb of reheat thrust. During WG760's third flight, on 11 August 1954, Roly Beamont created history by exceeding Mach 1 in level flight for the first time in a British aircraft, although this was not realised until the following day when the aircraft's speed was accurately computed. While the first P1A, as the type had been designated to avoid confusion with later versions, was employed primarily on performance and handling tests, WG763, which first flew on 18 July 1955, was fitted with some operational kit, including two 30mm Aden canon in the nose and, later, a 250gal jettisonable ventral auxiliary fuel tank subsequently adopted on most Service versions of the aircraft. A Napier Double Scorpion rocket motor in lieu of the ventral tank was also tested on WG763. Eventually the P1A achieved 1,010mph on the level (Mach 1.53), quite exceptional for such limited engine power, and without auto-stabilisation it proved to have excellent handling and manoeuvrability.

The P1B was the next step in the evolution of the design from research aircraft to service fighter, and the first example of the weapons system concept produced by the British aircraft industry, in which the fighter's radar and armament were integrated with the flying controls to provide a single-seat all-weather interceptor, capable of acquiring its target at considerable distances and destroying it with the high degree of certainty which until then had been the exclusive prerogative of American fighters. In many respects the P1B was a totally different aeroplane from the P1A, the most obvious external change being that the oval air intake of the latter was replaced by an annular intake with a fixed, cone-shaped centre body which conveniently housed the Ferranti intercept radar known as AIRPASS (Airborne Interception Radar Pilot Attack System) or AI 23 in service. The Sapphires were replaced by two Rolls-Royce Avons, each developing around 14,000lb thrust with reheat, giving a power-to-weight ratio close to unity. To afford the pilot better visibility the cockpit was raised and blended into a long dorsal spine which carried many essential services to the aft section of the aircraft. Lateral air brakes were added to each side of the rear fuselage, revised flaps (containing extra fuel) were fitted, changes were made to the undercarriage, with the main wheels incorporating thin tyres with the incredibly high pressure of 280psi. A pylon-mounted de Havilland Blue Jay (later, Firestreak) infra-red homing missile was positioned on each side of the nose as primary armament, in addition to two Aden guns. The missiles could be interchanged with alternative packs of either two more Adens or 48 unguided 2in rockets. A slightly taller fin of greater area was also introduced to counteract reduced stability of the two Firestreak missiles.

November 1956 saw the initial RAF orders placed, and on 4 April 1957 'Bee' took the first of three P1B prototypes, XA847, on its initial outing, exceeding

Mach 1.2 in the process. Coincidentally the government chose the very same day to publish its infamous Defence White Paper in which its architect, Duncan Sandys, stated that the missile era had now dawned and the manned interceptor fighter was soon to become an anachronism of the past. All of Britain's most promising fighter projects were hastily cancelled, and the P1 was reprieved only because of its advanced stage of development, although it did suffer much reduced orders from those which might otherwise have been anticipated.

Later, of course, the misguided politicians had to admit that (once again) they had got it wrong, but by then their meddling had caused irreparable damage to Britain's defences and aircraft industry, from which neither has ever been allowed to fully recover. On 23 October 1958 the P1B was officially christened the Lightning by the Chief of Air Staff, ending much deliberation during which several other names, including 'Excalibur', had also been proferred. Prototoype XA847 was used for engine development including testing with the Double Scorpion rocket motor, while the other two, XA853 and 856, were involved with weapons trials and operational equipment evaluation. This development programme was greatly accelerated by the order for 20 additional pre-production aircraft, a unique and long-overdue departure from previous British practice. Serialled XG307-313 and 325-337, the first flew on 3 April 1958, powered by RA24R Avons, rated at 14,430lb with reheat. During the next few years those pre-production aircraft were engaged in the evolution of the Lightning, testing a variety of features before their incorporation in new marks. One such feature, first tried on XG310, was the enlargement of the fin and rudder by 30%, henceforth to become standard on all 'first generation' Lightnings.

The first of 19 full-production Lightning F1s took to the air on 29 October 1959, and the next month saw the first deliveries of the type to the RAF, when XG334-336 of the pre-production batch went to the Air Fighting Development Squadron (AFDS) at Coltishall, Norfolk, and in December the Lightning received its official release for service use by the Controller of Aircraft. On 5 March 1960 the RAF lost the first (of many) Lightnings when XG334 'A'/AFDS suffered hydraulic failure over the North

Below: An early production Lightning F1, actually the third example (XM137) built to the full-production standard, seen at RAF Waddington in September 1961 in the markings of the Coltishall-based Air Fighting Development Squadron.
/ Roger Lindsay

Above: Another early Lightning F1, XM143, in the colourful markings of No 226 OCU at RAF Middleton St George in October 1963 — a red and white fin and fuselage spine with an appropriate St George's Cross badge. / *Roger Lindsay*

Sea and crashed near Wells-next-the-Sea, in Norfolk. This loss was made good on 14 May when the AFDS received XM135, the first full-production Lightning F1 to be issued to the RAF. This particular aircraft was destined to have the longest career of any F1, serving with seven different units until its final flight on 20 November 1974 from 60 MU, Leconfield, to Duxford where it now forms part of the historic aircraft collection of the Imperial War Museum. By far the most eventful moments during its 1,343 flying hours were those in 1965 when it was inadvertently taken-off by an engineering officer who was conducting engine runs and taxying tests at 33 MU, Lyneham. The officer involved had been a pilot several years earlier, when his last flying experience had been on 120mph Chipmunks, and so his involuntary transition to the Lightning was somewhat hair raising! Since the aircraft's ejection seat was inoperative he had little alternative but take XM135 around the circuit, and after several approaches he finally made a very good landing.

The first operational test for the Lightning came at the end of May 1960 when six F1s of the AFDS, operating from Leconfield, took part in the annual air defence exercise, 'Yeoman', in which they achieved 'a satisfactory rate of interception'. This rather tongue-in-cheek assessment of their excellent results was probably occasioned by the realisation that serviceability could have been better. Poor serviceability tended to afflict the Lightning during its early service career, and this applied to No 74 Squadron which became the first operational squadron to re-equip with the type when XM165 was delivered to Leconfield on 29 June 1960 while the squadron's home base, Coltishall, received attention prior to the introduction of large-scale Lightning operations. The squadron began conversion from its Hunter F6s aided by the AFDS, and it was not until 14 July that a No 74 Squadron pilot, appropriately the South African CO, Sqn Ldr J. F. G. Howe, flew the Lightning, by which time the squadron was back at Coltishall. Transition from the 720mph Hunter to Mach 2+ Lightning proved surprisingly trouble-free, and No 74 was able to demonstrate a quartet of its new supersonic fighters during the Farnborough Air Display in September, operating them from Boscombe Down. By the end of the year it had its full complement of 12 Lightinings and was declared operational early in the New Year.

No 74 Squadron remained the only Fighter Command squadron solely equipped with the F1 version of the Lightning, and the first to perform formation aerobatics with the type. In the spring of 1961 the squadron formed a six-ship aerobatic team which gave several displays, including the Paris Air Show in June, and by borrowing four aircraft from the AFDS, it was able to increase the team and fly in diamond-nine formation at Farnborough in September. As the 'Tigers', No 74 represented Fighter Command during the 1962 aerobatic 'season', and gave displays in Sweden and Norway, and just prior to the Farnborough Show in September it initiated a colourful era among Lightning squadrons by painting the fins and spines of its aircraft glossy black.

On 28 January 1964 No 74 moved to Leuchars, Fife, where it re-equipped with later Lightnings from

Above: Lightning F1A, XM184, of No 111 Squadron's CO, Sqn Ldr George Black, in May 1964 — the aircraft carries his pennant on the fin as well as below the cockpit. The fin and spine colours were black and yellow.
/ Roger Lindsay

April onwards, enabling its F1s to be handed-down to second-line training units. In fact the 'Tigers' had already donated seven F1s to help establish No 226 (Lightning) Operational Conversion Unit which was formed at Middleton-St George on 1 June 1963 to train prospective Lightning pilots, and later also ran refresher and weapons-attack instructor courses. On 13 April 1964 No 226 OCU moved to Coltishall, later acquiring more ex-No 74 Squadron F1s until these were phased out of service early in 1965. Apart from three aircraft lent to No 111 Squadron in 1964, by far the longest spell of service by F1s was as high speed manned targets, operated by the Target Facilities Flights (TFFs) at Binbrook (initially part of the Fighter Command Trials Unit), Wattisham and Leuchars from 1966 until December 1973 when these units disbanded. Prior to their TFF role these aircraft were up-dated at 33 MU, Lyneham, where several F1s were prematurely scrapped in 1965, before 60 MU at Leconfield took over as the main RAF Lightning storage and major maintenance unit.

The next variant of the Lightning to see service was the F1A, which differed from its predecessor in possessing in-flight refuelling capability by virtue of a detachable probe which fitted beneath the port wing, an improved windscreen rain/ice dispersal system, UHF radio instead of VHF, and some revisions to internal equipment and wiring which resulted in the presence of an external cable duct along each side of the lower fuselage — featured on all subsequent marks. The first of 28 F1As, XM169, flew on 16 August 1960, and No 56 Squadron at Wattisham, Suffolk, became the first operational user with its receipt of XM172 on 14 December 1960, followed by No 111 Squadron at the same base in the spring of 1961. The F1A's ability to refuel in flight was extensively practised by these squadrons and in July 1962 a section of No 56's Lightnings flew non-stop from Wattisham to Akrotiri, Cyprus, taking on fuel from Valiant tankers. In June 1962 No 111 Squadron took part in a re-deployment exercise to RAF Germany, and later they sent a detachment of aircraft to Malta, which then went on to Libya, where, with Firestreaks replaced by a pack containing an additional pair of Aden cannon, their Lightnings conducted live air-to-ground firing over desert ranges close to their temporary base of El Adem. Meanwhile No 56 Squadron provided Fighter Command's 1963 aerobatic team of Lightnings, named 'The Firebirds' after the unit's phoenix badge, a distinctive colour scheme of scarlet fin, spine, wing and tailplane edges adding the finishing touches to an extremely impressive repertoire. Early in 1965 the Wattisham Wing re-equipped with later Lightnings thereby releasing Lightning F1As for No 226 OCU where they replaced F1s, and later supplemented the TFFs.

Thanks to the availability of simulators, a thorough training plan, and the relative experience of those first RAF pilots selected to fly the Lightning, the conversion from subsonic aircraft had gone well, although it was realised at an early stage in the development of the P1B that a dual-controlled trainer variant was desirable. Design of the two-seater, known as the P11, began in the summer of 1957, and the prototype, XL628, flew on 6 May 1959. This trainer was virtually identical to the F1 with the exception

Above: Lightning F1A, XM173 of No 56 Squadron at the time when the unit provided 'The Firebirds' aerobatic team. / *Roger Lindsay*

Above right: The initial dual-control trainer variant of the Lightning was the T4, featuring a wider front fuselage to accommodate the side-by-side cockpit seating arrangement. This example, was seen with the Lightning Conversion Squadron at RAF Middleton St George in September 1962. / *Roger Lindsay*

Right: Lightning F2, XN733, of No 92 Squadron at RAF Leconfield in July 1964. / *Roger Lindsay*

Below right: The first squadron to take delivery of the F3 version of the Lightning was No 74 at RAF Leuchars. One of their aircraft, XP754, is seen at the Scottish base in September 1966 with the unit's famous 'Tiger stripe' nose markings. / *Roger Lindsay*

that the forward fuselage was widened $11\frac{1}{2}$in to accommodate in an enlarged cockpit the side-by-side seating then in vogue with RAF trainers and partly derived from the two-seat Hunter T7. The changes caused the deletion of the upper Aden cannon, but otherwise the Lightning trainer, designated the T4, was as operationally competent as the F1, and only marginally slower. After the first prototype crashed in the Irish Sea on 1 October 1959 flight testing was resumed from 21st of the month when the second prototype, XL629, first flew. Thirty production T4s, based on the F1A rather than the F1, were ordered for the RAF, later reduced to 20, the first, XM966, flying on 15 July 1960. The Lightning Conversion Squadron (LCS) became the first recipient on 27 June 1962 when XM970 was delivered to Middleton-St George. The LCS became No 226 OCU a year later and adopted the shadow role and markings of No 145 Squadron until May 1972 when its F1As and T4s changed markings to those of No 65 Squadron, which remained until the OCU disbanded at Coltishall in September 1974 when the remaining T4s were scrapped. Operational squadrons flying Mark 1 or Mark 2 fighters each received at least one T4, the last of which saw service with Nos 19 and 92 Squadrons in Germany. Two former RAF T4s, XM989 and 992, were transferred in 1966 to the Royal Saudi Air Force with the designation T54.

The fourth Lightning variant to see squadron service was the F2, externally almost identical to the F1A, but beneath its skin lay several important improvements: Avon 210 engines with much needed fully-variable reheat instead of the four-stage reheat of earlier versions; a liquid oxygen system; automatic flight control; improved instrumentation and avionics; and a standby turbo-generator for dc electric supply — the small dorsal intake for this equipment providing the only easy means of identifying the F2 apart from the serial number.

The first F2 to fly, XN723, was airborne on 11 July 1961 but, in common with the Lightning production programme in general, an inordinate time elapsed before the first service unit took delivery, on 14 November 1962, when XN771 was handed over to the AFDS at Binbrook. Forty-four F2s were ordered but several were retained on development work and converted to later marks, so that only two operational squadrons used this mark — Nos 19 and 92 at Leconfield, which re-equipped from Hunters between November 1962 and May 1963. One F2, XN788, was temporarily lent to No 111 Squadron in 1964, enabling that unit to make the unique claim of being the only operational squadron simultaneously equipped with four marks of Lightning, the 1, 1A, 2 and 4. Also in 1964, No 92 Squadron took over the mantle of the RAF's official Lightning aerobatic team. Five former RAF F2s were exported to Saudi Arabia as F52s in 1966/67.

On 23 September 1965 No 19 Squadron moved to Gutersloh to become permantly established in RAF Germany; No 92 Squadron followed to Geilenkirchen

K
XM971
DANGER
KEEP CLEAR OF INTAKE
WHEN ENGINE IS RUNNING

L
XN733

M
XP754

on 29 December, but joined up again with No 19 at Gutersloh in February 1968. These squadrons maintained a Battle Flight at constant readiness every day in the year, to guard against incursions into Allied air space by Warsaw Pact aircraft which were based less than 100 miles away.

Similarly in Britain, pairs of Lightnings were held on Quick Reaction Alert (QRA) status 24hr/day and were frequently scrambled to investigate unidentified aircraft entering the UK Air Defence Identification Zone.

As the menace grew special QRA 'sheds', housing two aircraft, their pilots and groundcrew, were built at the western end of Lightning base runways. Most of the Soviet incursions were off Northern Scotland, providing RAF Leuchars with by far the most 'trade', and hence priority in re-equipment with the latest Lightning — the F3. No 74 Squadron took delivery of XP700, the first example to reach an operational squadron, on 14 April 1964.

The F3 was the hottest Lightning of all, with more powerful Avon 301 engines, each rated at 12,690lb thrust dry and 16,300lb with reheat, which were improved to give greater reliability, and conferred a power-to-weight ratio close to unity, with a corresponding improvement in acceleration and agility. But these benefits were achieved at the expense of endurance, limitation of which could cut down a sortie to as short as 35-40min. The F3 was easily identified by its new square cut fin (first tested on XG310) of 15% increased area, which gave a clue to a major advance in armament — the Red Top missile. In conjunction with new AI23B radar, the Red Top, although derived from the Firestreak, permitted collision-course interceptions. The aircraft's avionics were more sophisticated, too, including the installation of OR946 instrumentation. The upper pair of nose-mounted Aden guns were deleted from the F3, later considered to be a retrograde step.

The first of 70 Lightnings completed as F3s (although 10 were converted to later marks), XP693, flew on 16 June 1962, and as usual the AFDS was the first RAF user, when it accepted XP694/'R', on New Year's Day, 1964. Subsequently the F3 formed the major equipment of No 23 Squadron at Leuchars which started to re-equip in August 1964, Nos 111 and 56 Squadrons at Wattisham (December 1964 and February 1965, respectively) each of which emblazoned their super new interceptors with the most eye-catching markings ever seen on postwar RAF fighters. No 56's red and white chequerboard fins attracted the displeasure of persons in high places, however, and by the end of 1965 such exotic decor was banned, and markings were toned down to subdued uniformity. Earlier that summer 'Treble One' had put up an aerobatic team of 12 out of its 13 Lightnings, showing that on occasion the aircraft could maintain high serviceability. April 1967 saw No

This picture: A Lightning F3 of No 111 Squadron seen in 1969, mid-way through the unit's 10-year period of operations with this mark of the interceptor.
/ MoD, Crown Copyright

56 Squadron posted to Akrotiri to provide permanent air defence for Cyprus, its place being taken at Wattisham by No 29 Squadron which reformed on 1 May with F3s, mostly made available by the re-equipment of Nos 23 and 74 Squadrons at Leuchars with a later mark of Lightning (the F6).

The Lightning F3 continued in squadron service with the Wattisham Wing well into the 1970s: No 56 Squadron was re-equipped in August 1971; No 111 Squadron disbanded on 30 September 1974, though not before adding three F6s to its complement of F3s; and No 29 Squadron also closed shop as a Lightning unit on the last day of that year — although by then both squadrons had already been reformed in the air-defence role, equipped with the Phantom FGR2, which it must be admitted has much better armament, radar, and range than the Lightning, as well as a two-man crew. No 226 OCU also operated F3s, firstly as No 145 then as No 2T Squadron, and Nos 5 and 11 Squadrons still retain about three F3s on strength in addition to their main equipment of F6s. The last 'new' unit to fly F3s was the Lightning Training Flight (LTF) which shares Binbrook with Nos 5 and 11 Squadrons, and which added three Mk 3s to its inventory early in 1976.

A dual-controlled proficiency trainer version of the F3, designated Lightning T5, was produced by British Aircraft Corporation's (BAC) Bristol Division, the allocation of the programme to Filton being aimed to prevent unemployment there. Wg Cdr Jimmy Dell made the first T5 flight, from Filton, on 29 March 1962, the aircraft XM967 being a conversion from a T4. Also reworked from T4 standard was the second machine, XM966, from which Jimmy Dell and his observer were obliged to eject on 22 July 1965, subsequently being safely fished out of the Solway Firth by a Whirlwind helicopter.

A further 22 new-build T5s were produced for the RAF, the second aircraft, XS417, being the first to fly on 17 July 1964, with XS419 the first to reach an 'operational' unit on 20 April 1965, going to No 226 OCU, the prime user of this mark. A single example also went to each F3 or F6 squadron, and these were often used operationally, even taking their turn on

Right: Export Lightnings on the apron at BAC's Warton aerodrome, Lancs; the picture shows three F53s for Saudi Arabia (nearest camera) and three F53s for Kuwait. / *BAC*

Left: The two-seat trainer evolved from the F3 was the T5; XS417, is seen here in the markings of RAF Binbrook's Lightning Training Flight in July 1977. / *Roger Lindsay*

Below: Seen equipped with the Lightning's ingeniously positioned 'drop tanks', is No 11 Squadron's F6 XS934. / *Roger Lindsay*

Bottom: The upper surfaces of Lightning F2As serving in RAF Germany were painted Dark Green starting in mid-1972, the scheme shown on this F2A of No 19 Squadron. / *RAF Gutersloh*

QRA duty. Following the demise of No 226 OCU in September 1974, the T5s formerly flown by that unit's 2T Squadron were mostly transferred to Binbrook where some were stored, a few struck off charge, while several others formed C Flight of No 11 Squadron which temporarily fulfilled the conversion and continuation training role. One of these aircraft, XS452/'Y' formerly held at Akrotiri where it had been decorated with a pale pink fin and flamingo marking derived from that station's badge, had the distinction of becoming the first UK-based Lightning to flight-test the experimental introduction of camouflage on the type — a matt Dark Green applied to the upper surfaces in August 1975. Soon afterwards a matt Dark Grey scheme was tested on XS458, by which time C Flight had been expanded to establish the Lightning Training Flight. A camouflage pattern embracing both these colours was adopted as standard for British-based Lightnings in 1976.

The final new-build version of the Lightning for the RAF stemmed from the eventual realisation by the Air Staff that the aircraft's endurance and range were totally inadequate — not merely for domestic air defence, but more keenly in the matter of overseas reinforcement. Because the Lightning's narrow fuselage was already packed to the gunwales with engines, armament, controls, a pilot, and miles of wiring, the options open to BAC's designers to increase the fuel capacity were somewhat limited. The fifth production F3, XP697, was selected to be rebuilt as the prototype for the new long-range version, initially referred to as the F3* or F3A, but re-designated F6 prior to squadron service. The metamorphosis took more than a year to complete, and when on 17 April 1964 'Bee' Beamont took XP697 on its first airing over Filton, the onlookers

could readily appreciate why! In its new guise the belly tank had been enlarged to massive proportions to contain 600gal of fuel, yet it was skilfully area-ruled to create less drag than the original 250gal tank it replaced; this increased average sortie duration to about 1hr 10min and the greater weight called for take-offs with full reheat. The outer sections of the wings were kinked by extending the new-cambered leading edge, and incorporated wide chord tips which reduced drag by 20% and increased range at subsonic cruising speeds. (This modified wing had originally been tested on P1A WG760 years earlier, but government thinking at that time discouraged its development.) BAC's ingenuity went even further, for the F6's main spar was beefed-up to enable a streamlined, jettisonable 260gal fuel tank to be mounted above each wing; this unique installation was primarily intended to boost the ferry range of the aircraft for overseas re-deployments, since the tanks were not stressed for combat manoeuvres.

Sixty-two Lightning F6s were delivered to the RAF, the first, XR752, flying on 16 June 1965 and the last, XS938, on 30 June 1967. Once again the first customer for the new Lightning was the AFDS, when it received XR753 on 16 November 1965 at Binbrook, where it was renamed the Fighter Command Trials Unit (FCTU) on 1 February 1966. Meanwhile No 5 Squadron at the same base had begun to receive F6s, with the arrival of XR755 and 756 on 10 December 1965. All these early Binbrook aircraft were 'Interim F6s', and lacked the ability to carry over-wing tanks as well as some other minor equipment, a deficiency later rectified after the aircraft had been 'modded' by the manufacturers. When the FCTU disbanded on 30 June 1966 its four F6s were transferred to No 23 Squadron at Leuchars which gradually re-equipped with a mixture of Interim and full-production F6s, while its companion squadron at the Scottish base, No 74, began to receive the later version from August 1966. Toting over-wing tanks, several of No 74's F6s set about testing the new mark's endurance capabilities (and those of their pilots!) by orbiting the UK, frequently taking on nourishment from Marham-based Victor tankers; and in January 1967 four of the new F6s flew Leuchars-Akrotiri non-stop, replenished en route by the Victors. On 1 June that year No 74's unrivalled long-range experience with Lightnings reached fulfilment in Exercise Hydraulic — the rapid re-deployment of the squadron's entire complement of 13 F6s from Leuchars to their new base at Tengah, on Singapore Island, 9,250 miles away. Led by the CO, Wg Cdr Ken Goodwin, the squadron was fully operational at Tengah within five days of its departure from Scotland, having staged through Akrotiri, Cyprus, Masirah in the Persian Gulf, and Gan Island in the Indian Ocean with the support of Victor tankers.

No 11 Squadron, which had reformed at Leuchars with F6s on 1 April 1967, took over from No 74 Squadron, and the same year saw the introduction of several innovations to the Lightning, notably the addition of a light to the probe, which eased the task of in-flight refuelling at night. In March a spring-loaded arrester hook, fitted beneath the rear fuselage of an F6, had been successfully tested at Leuchars, and so the device was subsequently installed on most Mk 2, 2A, 3 and 5 aircraft.

Lightning F2A was the designation applied to the 31 F2s which were converted by BAC to incorporate some of the range improvements of the F6. Basically these mods comprised fitting the enlarged belly tank, square-cut fin and kinked wing, which, however, was not stressed for over-wing tanks. During 1968/69 Nos

Right: Lightning scramble! An F6 unsticks at Akrotiri, Cyprus during a practice alert. / *RAF (NEAF)*

Left: Lightning F6 XS929 of No 56 Squadron at RAF Wattisham in May 1975. / *Martin Horseman*

Below: Lightning tailpiece — a view showing some of the unique features of the aircraft's design, notably the arrangement of the twin engines one above the other. The aircraft in the photograph is an F3 of No 111 Squadron pictured during a deployment to Akrotiri in January 1974. / *RAF (NEAF)*

19 and 92 Squadrons gradually exchanged their F2s for F2As, which were well-liked by their pilots; each squadron retained one or two 'plain' F2s, used mainly on TFF duties. From May 1972 onwards the upper surfaces of the Gutersloh-based Lightnings were camouflaged matt Dark Green as part of a general toning-down of aircraft and installations in RAF Germany. By this time many of these aircraft had about 3,000 flying hours to their credit, generally far more than any other Lightnings in service, in part a reflection of their high utilisation and the good serviceability upon which Nos 19 and 92 Squadrons, took so much pride. Their age caused most of the F2As to be processed through 60 MU for re-wiring — a time consuming task and one which proved to be extremely costly, since within a comparatively short time these same aircraft were destined to be withdrawn from service. The disbandment of Nos 19 and 92 Squadrons took place on 1 January and 31 March 1977 respectively and new Phantom squadrons took over their 'number-plates'.

Small detachments of British-based Lightnings were also a frequent sight at RAF Gutersloh in the early 1970s, and some F6s even temporarily operated out of the *Luftwaffe* base at Fassberg, located close to the East German border where they practiced rapid reaction scrambles. From 1970 the majority of Lightning F6s were modified to carry a pair of 30mm Aden cannon with 120 rounds per gun in the forward compartment of the ventral tank, fuel being retained in the main, rear section. The addition of guns was felt desirable in view of the greatly increased number of interceptions of Soviet intelligence-gathering aircraft, as it enabled the Lightning pilots to 'warn-off' the Russians should serious confrontation ever occur — whereas the previous total reliance upon the fighter's all-missile armament precluded such an option.

The belly-tank cannon armament had first been introduced on the export version of the F6, designated F53, 34 of which were ordered by Saudi Arabia late in 1965 together with six T55 trainers, which differed from the T5 in possessing the enlarged belly tank of the F6 and the extended, cambered, kinked wing — refinements which the RAF could not afford to fit retrospectively to their Mk 5s! This contract was worth about £100 million, and included technical and training support by British civilian companies, including Airwork Ltd, and the prior delivery of former RAF aircraft comprising two T4s and five F2s (previously mentioned), two Hunter T7s, and pre-production Lightning Mk 1 XG313 used for ground instruction, while Royal Saudi Air Force (RSAF) pilots were trained on four T55s at No 226 OCU, Coltishall.

The F53's wing was strengthened to carry 1,000lb of ordnance on a pylon beneath each wing-tip, in addition to the over-wing hard points, and a special photographic reconnaissance pack could be fitted forward of the belly tank. An RAF Lightning F3, XR722, was converted to become the F53 prototype, in which configuration it first flew on 19 October 1966 bearing the 'B' class registration G-27-2, as well as the RSAF number 53-666. Similarly, T5 XS460 became the T55 prototype, flying on 31 January 1966 as 55-710. The bulk of deliveries to Saudi Arabia were made during 1967/68 by both civilian and serving RAF pilots, with several replacement aircraft following later as a result of early attrition. In RSAF service the Lightnings have equipped Nos 1, 2, and 6 Squadrons, based at Kharmis Mushait and Dhahran, and the surviving aircraft still provide the country's most formidable interceptor pending their intended replacement by F-15 Eagles. Kuwait also ordered two T55 and 12 F53 Lightnings which entered service during 1968, again backed by considerable training and technical support from Britain. Their operational service has almost drawn to a close with the arrival of replacement Mirage F1s from France.

There is little doubt that Lightning exports would have been substantially greater had the British government not shown such disinclination to develop the aircraft's potential from the outset. As early as 1957 West Germany was showing a keen interest, later shared by several other countries, including India.

August 1971 marked the beginning of the decline of the Lightning in RAF service, when No 74 Squadron disbanded in Singapore and passed on most of its F6s to No 56 Squadron at Akrotiri, Cyprus. The latter unit returned home to Wattisham in January 1975, and relinquished Lightnings on 28 June 1976, while No 23 Squadron at Leuchars followed suit on 31 October.

Though now largely superseded by the Phantom, the Lightning still flourishes with Nos 5 and 11 Squadrons and the LTF in its last retreat, appropriately RAF Binbrook — the airfield so closely associated with the early operational evaluation of the aircraft. For those pilots privileged still to fly the Lightning there can be few more satisfying, or demanding occupations. The classic 1965 RAF recruitment advertisement showing a young pilot about to clamber into the cockpit of his Lightning couldn't have expressed it more perfectly: 'Same old thing every day . . . excitement!' The typical Lightning squadron pilot still gets that excitement by flying up to four sorties a day (or night), which may be practice interceptions with another Lightning; or air combat training against a Harrier or perhaps an F-5E from the USAF's 'Aggressor' Squadron; or 'tanking' from a Victor; or being vectored by an airborne early-warning Shackleton to engage a Buccaneer streaking very low above the North Sea. Every now and then he gets to fire the Adens at a banner towed behind a No 100 Squadron Canberra, and once in a while he may do the same thing but against a setting of sun-soaked Cyprus. He will probably enjoy at least one exchange visit annually to another NATO fighter base in Europe, and once a year he may be permitted to fire a missile at a flare target trailed by a Jindivik off the Welsh coast. If he's really lucky he might just get the chance of scrambling to intercept a Soviet 'Bear', high above the icy northern seas, where his only link with far off land is the friendly voice of the radar controller through his earphones; after such an encounter there's more satisfaction than usual when the narrow tyres screech on to the runway at 165 knots beneath 15 tons of Lightning.

Sadly the Lightining can't go on for ever, but when its tyres have hit the runway for the last time this superlative fighter will be sure of a special place in British aviation history.

BOEING
707
N70700
BOEING

Boeing 707 Quarter-century

MARTIN HORSEMAN

Among the many aviation anniversaries recalled in 1979, there was none more significant in the history of civil air transport than the first flight 25 years ago of the Boeing 707 prototype — the Model 367-80. It was on 15 July 1954 that the forerunner of more than 3,500 Boeing jet airliners lifted-off from Renton Field, Washington, to usher in a new era in airliner design and performance. America's first jet transport was powered by four Pratt & Whitney JT3 turbojets contained in individual pods which were mounted beneath wings swept back at 35 degrees. Looking very much the technical innovation it was, compared with contemporary piston-engined, straight wing airliners, the sleek 'Dash 80' established a classic configuration for the future.

Boeing's initial studies into jet airliners began as early as 1946, the company evaluating turbojet (as well as turboprop)-powered versions of the military C-97 variant of its Model 337 — the Stratocruiser. Neither civil nor military interest was forthcoming in the various drawing board and wind tunnel projects of the late 1940s and early 1950s, but Boeing decided to proceed nonetheless, and announced in August 1952 that it was investing $16 million of its own funds to build the prototype of an entirely new jet transport.

Left: The airframe which inaugurated the Boeing 707 story, the Model 367-80, registered N70700, first flew on 15 July 1954 and was subsequently used as the test aircraft for many refinements of the design before its 'retirement' in 1972. / *Boeing*

Above: The USAF order for the air refuelling version of the Boeing four-jet transport was of vital significance in launching the production programme: s/n 63-7981 is a late production KC-135A and seen in November 1974 while serving with the 384th Air Refuelling Squadron based at McConnell AFB, Kansas — the nose artwork proclaims *Wichita — Center City, USA*. / *Martin Horseman*

Right: Boeing 707-320C Intercontinental, YI-AGE, of Iraqi Airways. The airline's attractive colour scheme seems to accentuate the long, lean lines of this largest member of the Boeing 707 family. / *Boeing*

Although the subsequent production aircraft were to be labelled Model 707, the prototype was designated the Model 367-80 — partly to maintain corporate security as to the scope of the project but also because many of the earlier design studies had evolved from advanced versions of the C-97, the Model 367. Thus it was that the new design became known as the 'Dash 80' to the Boeing production and technical personnel and as the '707' to the company sales force and the public.

After two years' work concealed in the Boeing production plant at Renton, the hangar doors were opened on 15 May 1954 and the prototype was rolled out for inspection by thousands of employees and visitors. Finished in a chocolate and yellow colour scheme and bearing the appropriate registration N70700, the Dash 80 totally belied its Model 367 designation. Aerodynamically, the prototype was closer to the B-47 Stratojet, the first example of which had flown as early as December 1947, than to the C-97. Although consideration had been given to mounting the engines in double pods, as on the inboard pylons of the B-47, the powerplants were installed in single pods for safety and structural benefits — in a double pod the failure of one engine might compromise the continued operation of the adjacent unit, and four pods provided better weight distribution along the wing. The B-47 and B-52 type 'bicycle' landing gear was supplanted by an entirely new 'tricycle' arrangement undercarriage, the main wheels of which were to retract inwards from the centre wing stub into stowage bays in the lower fuselage.

Just how much of a risk Boeing had shouldered in developing its new jet transport as a private venture was to become obvious in the months following the roll-out and initial flight testing of the Dash 80 as the company waited... and waited for airline interest to materialise in firm orders. It was not until October 1955, more than year after the prototype's first flight, that Pan American placed the landmark order for 20 707s which prompted the subsequent avalanche of orders from major domestic US and international carriers.

In the interim, however, Boeing's investment in the programme had been safeguarded by the reawakening of USAF Strategic Air Command interest in the design as a follow-on to the KC-97 series of air refuelling tanker/transports. Two months after the Dash 80's maiden flight, an initial batch of 29 tanker versions of the aircraft was ordered by the USAF: to Boeing the air refuelling variant became the Model 717-100 while the Air Force designated it the KC-135A Stratotanker.

Iraqi airways
YI-AGE

Below: KC-135A Stratotankers crowd the flight line area at Barksdale AFB, Louisiana during the November 1974 USAF Strategic Air Command Bombing and Navigation Competition, 'Giant Voice'. The larger picture shows a tanker of the 908th Air Refuelling Squadron/449th Bomb Wing from Kincheloe AFB, Michigan. / *Martin Horseman*

Inset right: Close-up of another KC-135A participant at 'Giant Voice 74' (s/n 63-8027) from the 305th ARS/305th ARW at Grissom AFB, Indiana. / *Martin Horseman*

Top: The first Boeing 707 to enter airline service was N709PA, the third production -120; *Clipper America*, is seen during its first visit to Heathrow that year.
/ Peter Clifton

Above: Also an early customer for the 707 was 'Australia's overseas airline', Qantas, whose initial aircraft were 707-138s. Shown here is the first of the type, VH-EBA *City of Melbourne*, but seen after modification to turbofan-powered, -138B standard.
/ Peter Clifton

The KC-135 was similar in design to the 707 prototype but fitted with the Boeing-developed flying boom attached to the underside of the rear fuselage; the fuel was all located in lower deck and wing tanks, and a single large door was incorporated in the left-side forward fuselage allowing access to an unobstructed main deck for cargo and/or personnel transport.

The preliminary order for the KC-135 was followed by others which were to lead to an eventual procurement of well over 800 military examples of the 707. While most of the aircraft were acquired as tankers, some have been drastically modified to fulfil a variety of special missions, and in those roles their 707-shape has been considerably revised by the addition of sensors, radars and other scanners, and communications equipment.

Meanwhile the commercial airliner programme had got underway, the first production model of the aircraft being the Boeing 707-120. The -120 series was designed primarily for US transcontinental sectors (coast to coast) but was capable also of trans-Atlantic operations. Larger and heavier than the Dash 80 prototype, and with more powerful engines (P&W JT3Cs of 12,500lb thrust each), the initial 707-120 was rolled-out at Renton in October 1957. Pan American put the type into service on its New York to Paris route on 26 October 1958 (incidentally, some 16 months after the first KC-135 had been delivered to the USAF).

Top: An example of the initial production version of the long range -320 Intercontinental model of the 707. Air France placed one of the largest orders, and the photo shows their F-BHSB, *Chateau de Chambord*. / *Boeing*

Above: The first Boeing 707s powered by turbofans were the -420 aircraft equipped with Rolls-Royce Conway engines: photo shows a British Airways 707-436, G-ARRC. / *British Airways*

Right: The Boeing 720, originally designated the 707-020, was a shorter range version of the 707 developed from the early -120 series. Although similar in outward appearance to the 707, the 720 was a major re-design, and it first entered service in July 1960. Seen here is American Airlines' N7527A. / *Boeing*

The 707-120s later inaugurated US coast to coast services with American Airlines, first flying the New York-Los Angeles route on 25 January 1959. The model was also procured by the USAF which bought the -120 under the designation VC-137A as a VIP transport. Another special version was the 707-120B, with a 10ft shorter fuselage to reduce weight and improve range performance. A follow-on series to the initial -120 variant was the 707-220, identical in size but with increased thrust JT4A-3 engines of 15,800lb each.

The largest members of the Boeing 707 'family' were to be the so-called 'Intercontinentals', the long-range airliners capable of carrying over 200 passengers (under normal conditions, that is. A refugee flight by a 707-320 during the 1960 crisis in the Congo, carried over 300 people from Leopoldville to Brussels!). These 'stretched' 707s were the -320 and -420 series which featured larger wing areas, longer fuselages and increased fuel capacity; the -320 was powered by the same engine type as the -220, while the -420 was fitted with four Rolls-Royce Conway engines each of 17,500lb thrust.

Another development of the Boeing 707 was the lighter weight Boeing 720 (sometimes also referred to as the 707-020) aimed at airline requirements for shorter range sectors. The new model had a reduced fuselage length, revised leading edge flaps spanning the entire wing, lighter structural weight, a new inboard wing profile and less fuel capacity. These changes combined to produce a sparkling performance in the required role, conferring a higher maximum speed and the capability of operation from shorter runways. United Airlines in the US was the first customer for the 720, and the aircraft initially went into service in July 1960.

Further performance gains were to accrue to the 707-320 series and the 720 from the programme which married the P&W JT3D turbofan of 18,000lb thrust to these established models. The new powerplants plus new wing-tips and high lift flaps enabled the -320B, for example, to fly 20% further than the -320 with the same payload. The USAF's VC-137As were re-engined with turbofans to become VC-137Bs, while 707-320Bs were supplied to the Air Force under the designation VC-137C.

Another modified version of the -320 series was the 320C, the 'C' suffix indicating a convertible cargo/passenger variant of the turbofan-powered -320B equipped with a strengthened floor and a side fuselage door for main deck cargo pallets. In an all-passenger configuration, the -320Cs can carry up to 219 passengers, and the type first entered service with Pan American in June 1963.

Below: The ultimate version of the Intercontinental 707 was the -320C, turbofan powered and with the 'C' denoting the availability of a customer option to operate it in a cargo or convertible passenger/cargo configuration. Nigeria Airways' 5N-ABJ is seen on a pre-delivery test flight. / *Boeing*

Bottom: The turbofan-powered version of the 720 was the 720B, here represented by D-ABOH of Lufthansa. / *Boeing*

Above: The C-135A Stratolifter was ordered by the USAF's MATS as a long-range transport. Photo shows the first example of the type, s/n 60-0356 which was a production line KC-135A completed to C-135A configuration. Full production standard Stratolifters were equipped with the taller 707-type fin. / *Boeing*

Right: This turbofan-powered EC-135C is one of a number of such conversions from KC-135B standard (note the air refuelling boom) used as airborne command posts by the USAF. / *Boeing*

Far right: The prototype AWACS aircraft, a converted 707-320B mounting an above fuselage radar installation. / *Boeing*

After Boeing had delivered several hundred KC-135 Stratotankers to Strategic Air Command, the military interest in the programme broadened when, in 1961, the aircraft was ordered by the predecessor of today's USAF Military Airlift Command (MAC) — namely, the Military Air Transport Service (MATS). The MATS requirement for an up-to-date inter-theatre, passenger/cargo jet transport was met initially by the Boeing Model 707-157, or C-135A, almost identical to the KC-135 but with a larger fin and without the Stratotanker's air refuelling capability. The subsequent C-135B variant was equipped with P&W turbofan engines similar to those powering the 'B' model 707s and 720s.

Numerous KC-/C-135s were extensively modified after delivery into special purpose aircraft for weather reconnaissance (WC-135), electronic and radar reconnaissance (RC-135), airborne command and communications duties (EC-135), monitoring nuclear bomb tests (NKC-135) and other roles. In most of these cases the pedigree of the original design is still very evident, but the aircraft have sprouted a variety of extra appendages in the form of radomes, sensor housings and aerials. The most remarkable, and recent, transformation is the modified Boeing 707-320B airframe equipped with an above-fuselage rotating radome, or rotodome, housing a long-range surveillance radar. The aircraft, which entered service with USAF Tactical Air Command in 1977, is designated the E-3A Sentry: its role is that of an airborne warning and control system, or AWACS for short. The AWACS radar system is capable of detecting and tracking aircraft flying at high or low altitudes, over both land or water, and the surveillance radar coupled with extensive on-board avionics equipment enables the mission crew to relay early warning of hostile air operations and to coordinate the response of friendly forces.

By the end of September 1978, Boeing had taken orders for 934 aircraft in all versions of the 707/720 series, and only the ultimate model of the aircraft, the -320C, remained in production — at a rate of one aircraft every two months.

None but the most visionary could have appreciated the developments which were to ensue in the 25 years after the completion, roll-out and first flight of the Model 367-80 in 1954 — the success of not just the KC-135 and 707 programmes but the establishment of a tri-jet and twin-jet lineage in the form of the Boeing 727 and 737 families, and the culminating colossus in the 707 mould, the Boeing 747 Jumbo-jet. In the evolution of these later Boeing jet transports, the Model 367-80 prototype played an important role as a flying test-bed for the many aerodynamic and structural refinements which were developed. New wing platforms and aerofoils, powerplant modifications, weather radars, entirely novel wing leading edge and trailing edge flap systems, rough field landing gear, and an aft-mounted engine pod for the 727 design were among the features first tested on the Dash 80. It was small wonder that this most tested and pioneering example of a now famous design was described as 'one of the 12 most significant aircraft of all time' when it was accepted into honourable retirement by the Smithsonian Institution in 1972.

Sidelights on

PHILIP J. R. MOYES

'A four-engined Whitley with a Wellington's tail' was how World War II aircraft spotters in Britain sometimes described the Short Stirling bomber and, when one thinks about it, that description was fairly apt. RAF Bomber Command's first four-engined 'Big Stick' was certainly a very angular aeroplane — though it did have some noticeable curves in the tips of its wings and tail surfaces — and even if its wing planform was not quite the barndoor-like affair of the Whitley or 'Wombat', its low aspect ratio did seem to make the huge railway coach of a fuselage all the more ungainly.

From the operational viewpoint the low aspect ratio wing was a serious handicap to the Stirling's ceiling, but it was something that was forced upon Shorts' design team by the Air Ministry, who, in their B12/36 specification, decreed that the span should not exceed 100ft to conform with contemporary hangar dimensions. Shorts initially wanted to give the big bomber a wing similar to that of their Sunderland flying-boat and spanning 112ft, and had they been allowed to do so the Stirling saga might have been a

the Stirling

Above: Before proceeding with the prototype Stirling, Shorts built this half-scale wooden flying model powered by Pobjoy Niagaras and accommodating a pilot and an observer in tandem.

Above left: The fourth production Rochester-built Stirling BI. Points of interest are the Sky finish on the undersurfaces, the presence of spinners on the propellers and the small vane-like protrusion beneath the rear fuselage under the roundel — this an indication that a ventral turret was installed.

Left: The Stirling was a victim of its own specification, because of which its main bomb bay was divided into narrow compartments suitable for nothing bulkier than 2,000lb armour-piercing bombs (not shown here).
/ All photos with this article were supplied by the Author

far happier one. As it was, the Stirling could attain little more than 12,000ft with a full bomb load. Even with the reduced bomb loads that it normally carried in service, it was hard put to reach much more than 16,000ft on most occasions — which was still far below par. Another unfortunate aspect of the Stirling was that its bomb bay, although 42ft 7in long, was sectionalised longitudinally in such a way that it could not accommodate anything larger than 2,000lb bombs, this again being a drawback inherent in the original 1936 design specification.

All in all, then, the Stirling was a compromise from the word 'go', and although it was certainly a far better weapon than any of the trio of 'first generation' bombers with which Bomber Command went to war — namely the Hampden, Wellington and Whitley — it was never anywhere near so successful as those two other 'second generation' heavies which followed it into service: the Halifax and that queen of the fleet, the mighty Lancaster. Nevertheless, it did a sterling job (if readers will forgive the pun) and today there are many ex-bomber crews who still remember the old 'kite' with great affection.

The Stirling was a product of the RAF expansion scheme, which was inaugurated in the mid-1930s to help meet the growing threat of war with Nazi Germany. The B12/36 specification was issued to the British aircraft industry in July 1936 and following the Air Ministry's acceptance of their tender, Shorts received a contract for two prototypes and, soon afterwards, an initial production order for 200 'straight off the drawing board'. Before the prototypes flew, however, Shorts built a half-scale wooden flying model (the S31) powered by Pobjoy Niagara engines for evaluation. Accommodating a pilot and observer in tandem, this mini-Stirling first flew from Rochester (Kent) Airport on 19 September 1938, in conditions of great secrecy, and both the firm's and the subsequent A&AEE Martlesham Heath flight test reports were quite encouraging, although the A&AEE recommended a three-degree increase in wing incidence for the full-sized Stirling to shorten take-off and landing runs. However, the need to meet delivery dates resulted in the increased ground angle having to be achieved by lengthening the landing gear — a modification also incorporated into the S31. The Stirling prototype (L7600) eventually took the air on 14 May 1939 but on landing at Rochester one of its brakes seized, whereupon the stalky undercarriage collapsed and the aircraft bellied-in and became a total write-off. This was a severe blow, as the second prototype was not ready to start trials until 21 November. Fitted with a strengthened undercarriage it made a successful first flight on 3 December, though the undercarriage was locked down on this occasion lest bad luck should strike again. Happily it did not, and thereafter the flight test programme was able to proceed on schedule.

Shorts' first production aircraft (N3635) flew on 7 May 1940 and in July deliveries of Stirling Is to the RAF began. In the following month, when a second source — Short & Harland of Queen's Island, Belfast* — was also about to start deliveries, the Stirling began to enter service with Bomber Command. The re-formed No 7 Squadron at the 4 Group base of Leeming, near Northallerton, Yorkshire, was the first recipient and for the record its first machine was N3640, which was allotted on 2 August.

At this juncture a few words about the Stirling I's fuselage layout might be useful. Entry was via a door in the port side of the rear fuselage, and in the long walk forward to the cockpit one passed the retractable

* Short & Harland was formed in 1936 and was jointly owned by Short Bros and the shipbuilding firm of Harland & Wolff. Before building Stirlings it built Bristol Bombays and Handley Page Herefords.

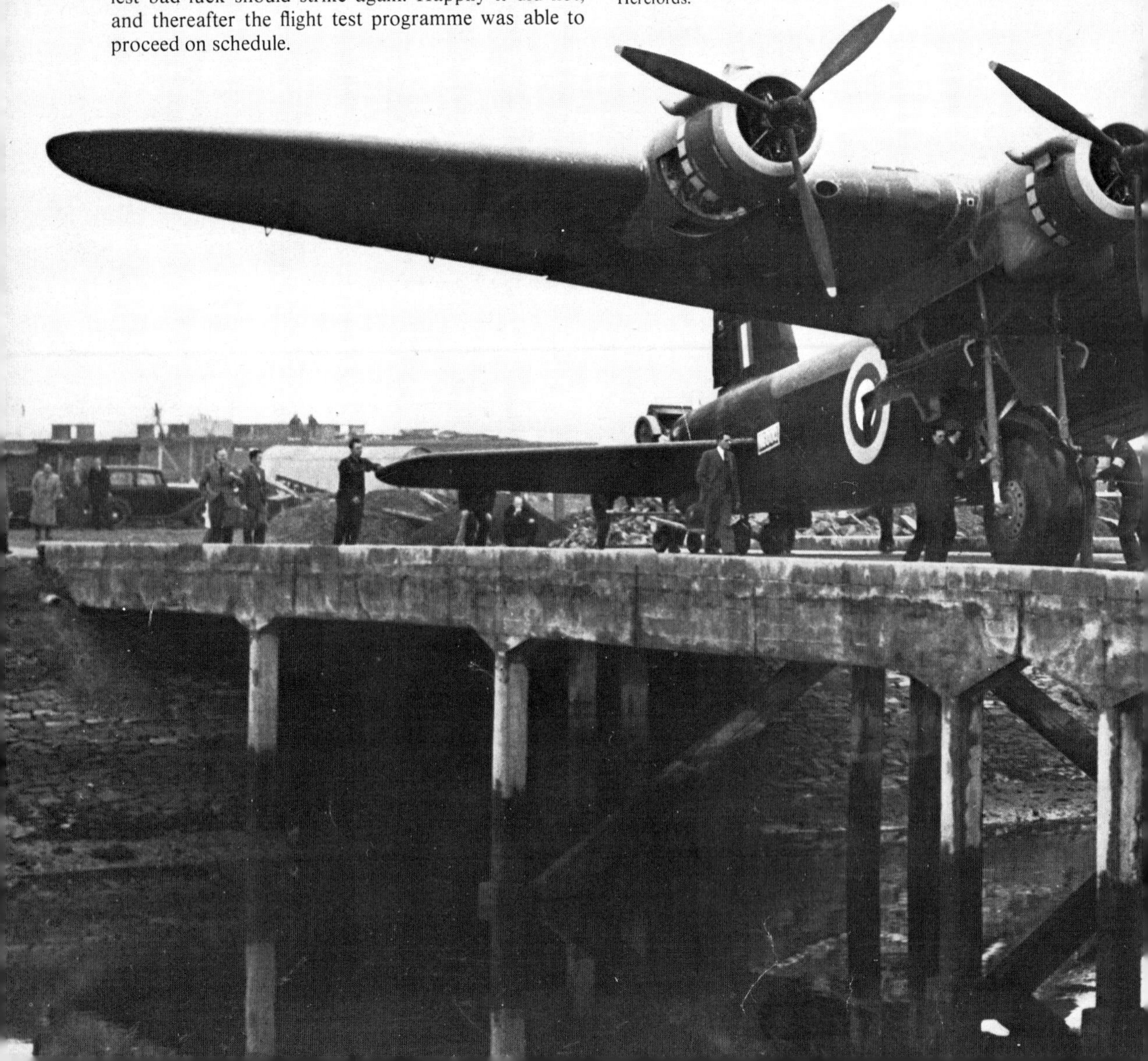

Frazer-Nash 'dustbin' ventral turret, the emergency mechanism for the undercarriage, the same for the huge Gouge-type flaps, the priming and starting boxes for the four Bristol Hercules engines (though the pilot himself pressed the buttons), the cocks for the fuel tanks, dump valves, balance cocks, a rest bunk, an easy chair, a navigator's desk and chair, the radio compartment and the flight engineer's panel. The cockpit had roomy seats for two pilots, each with control column, wheel and rudder bar, and between the seats was a control bank containing the throttles, constant-speed controls, mixture levers, undercarriage selector, landing light adjuster and brake lever. In the roof were the main fuel cocks to the carburettor, slow-running cut-offs, tail trimming and rudder trimming cranks. In the V of the windscreen were the flap operation switch and indicator. On the instrument panel were the usual flying instruments plus four boost gauges and four rev indicators. In the extreme nose was the bomb aimer's compartment situated under the floor of the pilots' compartment and the nose gun turret. In this compartment was also a trap-door by which the crew could enter or leave the aircraft. In the rear end of the fuselage was the tail turret, reached by a catwalk and supplied with ammunition which ran in rails from magazines located high up on the port side of the fuselage just aft of the bomb bay.

The twin-Browning ventral 'dustbin' turrets fitted to the early Mk I Stirlings proved too cramped for continuous occupation and, in addition to increasing drag when lowered in flight, had a nasty habit of slipping down through leakage of the hydraulic non-return valves when vibrated during taxying, causing the guns to scrape along the ground. These turrets, therefore, were removed and the early production Stirling Is were fitted instead with single pivoted

This picture: The first Belfast-built Stirling BI, N6000, crossing Connswater bridge at Queen's Island en-route from the factory to neighbouring Sydenham airfield for test flying.

Top: First Stirling squadron was No 7, one of whose original Mk Is is shown. D-Donald did in fact take part in the unit's first operational mission with the type — an attack by three Stirlings on oil storage tanks at Rotterdam, Holland, on the night of 10/11 January 1941.

Above: In this view of one of No 7 Squadron's early Stirlings, a Spitfire parked under the port wing lends scale.

Brownings firing through side windows. Later, twin beam guns became standard, but these proved inadequate in combat with the result that they, in turn, were replaced by a twin-Browning Frazer-Nash dorsal turret similar to that of the Avro Manchester and Blackburn Botha. The new turrets appeared in service in June 1941.

To return now to No 7 Squadron. The unit moved in October 1940 to Oakington, a 3 Group airfield in Cambridgeshire, from whence it eventually flew its first operational mission with Stirlings on the night of 10/11 January 1941 when three aircraft dropped a total of 46 500lb bombs on oil storage tanks at Rotterdam. Among targets visited soon afterwards was the French Atlantic port of Brest, mainly because of the presence there of the notorious German battle-cruisers *Scharnhorst* and *Gneisenau*, or 'Salmon and Gluckstein' as they were known to RAF bomber crews. Oakington, then a grass airfield without concrete runways, became a quagmire about this time and, as a result, No 7's operations were temporarily mounted from another 3 Group airfield at Rowley Mile on the famous racecourse at Newmarket. However, this airfield had a hazardous bank — the ancient fortification known as the Devil's Dyke — not far from the end of its main grass runway and thus the crews were greatly relieved when Oakington became usable again.

Berlin was attacked by No 7 Squadron on 17/18 April and that same month saw a second squadron convert to Stirlings — No 15 Squadron at Wyton which began ops with a raid on the 'Big City' on the night of 30 April/1 May. By the end of 1941 more than 150 Stirlings had been delivered to the RAF and a third squadron, No 149, was operational. Gradually, as other 3 Group squadrons converted from Wellingtons to Stirlings, the Short bomber became the group's standard equipment. The Stirlings were frequently operated by day as well as by night during 1941, their first day raid being against Emden on 27 April. In a day raid on the *Scharnhorst* at La Pallice in the afternoon of 23 July, one of two Stirlings of No 15 Squadron which reached the target area (the other bombed an objective elsewhere) was attacked by

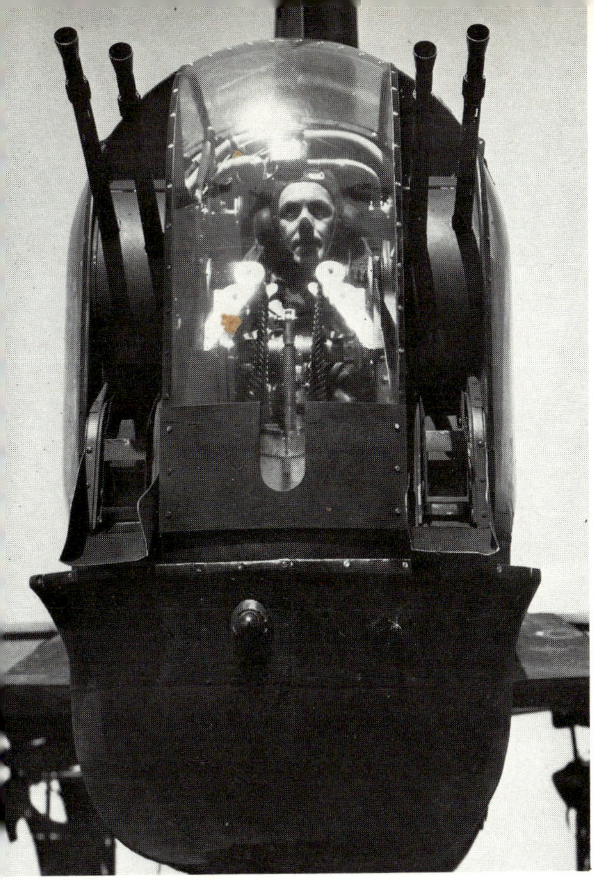

German fighters and had to be ditched in the sea. Three aircraft of No 7 Squadron also reached the target area and a bomb from one of these scored a direct hit on the stern of the *Scharnhorst*. This same Stirling (N6037) was attacked by two Messerschmitt Bf109s but both were shot down by the rear gunner, who also damaged a third.

December 1941 saw Stirlings of Nos 7 and 15 Squadrons, carrying second pilots and wireless operators from No 109 Anson/Wellington Squadron whose job was developing radar aids and RCM apparatus, using an early blind-bombing device known as *Trinity* (a rudimentary form of *Oboe*) in a series of attempts to bomb *Scharnhorst* and *Gneisenau* at Brest. Similar attacks were mounted in the New Year.

Time and again during operations Stirlings showed themselves to be capable of absorbing heavy battle damage yet still keep flying. An excellent example of

Left: 'Tail-end Charlie' in his Frazer-Nash turret armed with four .303in Brownings.

Below: Lady MacRobert, of Dounside, Tarland, Aberdeenshire, who lost three sons — two in the RAF during WW2 — generously contributed £25,000 towards the cost of a Stirling and an aircraft (Stirling BI N6086) was duly named *MacRobert's Reply*; and, as LS-F, flew with No 15 Squadron from RAF Wyton, Huntingdonshire, where is is seen here overflying some of the unit's other Stirlings.

this was seen on 27/28 June 1942, when Stirling I N3751 of No 214 Squadron, from Stradishall in Suffolk, took part in a raid against Bremen. The aircraft, captained by Sgt F. M. Griggs, an Australian, had bombed the target and was crossing the Dutch frontier on its way home when two twin-engined 'twin-tailed' fighters, apparently Messerschmitt Bf110s, attacked simultaneously. The bomber's front and mid-upper gunners retaliated and one night fighter was driven off and the other shot down and seen to crash. During this phase, the Stirling had one engine, its intercom, radio and electrical systems put out of action, the rear gunner was killed and the wireless operator wounded. Griggs struggled to keep his damaged aircraft on course but as he crossed the Dutch coast his navigator spotted two Bf109s diving to attack. The front gunner, who was giving first aid to the wireless operator, was barely warned in time by the navigator, who had to run down the fuselage to give the alarm. Both the 109s were shot down into the sea, but the Stirling had taken still more punishment and had dropped to 8,000ft where flak ships found it an easy target. Soon afterwards another 109 attacked and in manoeuvring to escape from it Griggs lost control of his crippled bomber which started to dive. He was nearly at sea level when he regained flying attitude and struggled across the North Sea on his three remaining engines. Above the airfield a second engine caught fire, but the flames were extinguished and with only the two port engines working Griggs managed to crash-land without injuring any member of the crew.

Occasionally, the English weather caused individual squadrons of Bomber Command more casualties than either enemy flak or fighters. On 14 July 1941, for example, six Stirlings of No 7 Squadron were detailed for a raid on Hanover. The results were good but the weather clamped down during the return trip. Only one of the six bombers managed to land back at Oakington. Of the others, one (N6022) ran out of fuel, was abandoned by its crew and crashed at Newton Flotman in Norfolk; another (N6033), also abandoned by its crew after running out of fuel, crashed in the centre of Northampton much to the disgust of the Chief Constable, who rang operations to say 'I can't have this' and two more (N6036 and N7434) sustained damage in landing away from base. Several of the men who baled out were injured and one was killed.

Arrangements to build Stirlings in Canada were made in 1941 and a contract was placed for 140 Stirling BIIs powered by 1,600hp Wright Cyclone

Left: A Belfast-built Stirling BIII, BF509, pictured during a test flight in March 1943.

Above: ***Rara avis*** **— one of the two examples of the Wright Cyclone-powered Stirling BII, both of which were converted from BIs to become prototypes of the proposed Canadian-built Mk II.**

R-2600-A5B engines. Two Mk II prototypes were produced at Rochester by converting Mk Is N3657 and N3711 and flown in August and December 1941, but soon afterwards the Canadian contract was cancelled and the Mk II never entered production. Further projected production of the Mk II at the South Marston (Wiltshire) shadow factory, which was already building the Mk I, was also abandoned.

A third and final bomber mark of Stirling appeared in 1942: the B Mk III (1,635hp Hercules XVI engines with underslung oil coolers), the prototypes of which were converted from Mk Is R9188 and R9309. The BIII was generally similar to the BI srs III (which, unlike the BI srs I and II, had complete Bristol-designed powerplant assemblies or 'power eggs' including oil tanks and engine-driven accessories), minor differences being the installation of a Lancaster-type FN50 dorsal turret (also seen on some Mk I srs IIIs), larger fuel tanks, and a revised interior layout with fewer oval windows in the rear fuselage. The BIII weighed 43,200lb empty and had a maximum all-up weight of 70,000lb. Maximum speed was 270mph at 14,500ft, normal cruising speed 200mph at 15,000ft and service ceiling 18,000ft. It could fly 2,010 miles with 3,500lb of bombs or 590 miles with 14,000lb. Stirling BIII production was undertaken at Rochester, South Marston, Belfast and the Austin shadow factory at Longbridge (Birmingham), all of which had previously built the Mk I. Stirling IIIs re-equipped existing Stirling squadrons, though by no means always completely, and were also issued to five new squadrons which formed in 3 Group during the summer of 1943.

Meanwhile, early in 1942 the Stirlings of 3 Group had been fitted with the new medium-range radio aid to navigation and target identification known as *Gee*, the operational use of which had been pioneered by Wellingtons of No 115 Squadron the previous August. *Gee* was put into general operational use by Bomber Command in March 1942 — although the force was still only in the early stages of being equipped with it — and it made a major contribution to the success of the first 'Thousand Bomber' raid, on Cologne, on the night of 30/31 May 1942. *Gee*-equipped Stirlings and Wellingtons formed the first wave of the attack; they navigated by *Gee* until their crews were close enough to identify the target visually in the bright moonlight, and their incendiary bombs started fires which were easily recognised by the two subsequent waves. The standard of accuracy was high and 3 Group's AOC, AVM J. E. A. Baldwin, who personally accompanied his crews in one of the first wave Stirlings, reported fires within half a mile of the aiming point even before his aircraft arrived on the scene. The raid completely destroyed 600 acres of Cologne's built-up area — almost as much as all previous devastation in German towns added together.

In August 1942 the original Stirling squadron, No 7, was honoured by being selected, together with three non-Stirling squadrons, to form the nucleus of the Path Finder Force (PFF) and was soon helping to lead

Left: On the line — Stirling Is of No 7 Squadron at RAF Oakington, Cambridgeshire. Note the small squadron code letters and the two distinct types of dorsal turrets.

main force squadrons as far afield as Genoa, Turin and Milan in Northern Italy. On one raid against Turin the weather was so bad that only two Stirlings out of the eight detailed from No 7 Squadron reached their target. In the vicinity of the Alps the cloud bank was over 20,000ft, and the two Stirlings flew through it on dead reckoning to emerge almost directly over Turin. Only the aircraft skippered by Flt Lt J. F. Barron, a New Zealander, completed its mission, the other being shot down over the target. During a subsequent raid on Munich, Barron's Stirling was twice attacked by night fighters. The rear gunner drove one off and probably destroyed it, but the other, a Junkers Ju88, made repeated attacks, raking the bomber with machine-gun fire. Parts of the wing and tailplane were torn away and the fuel supply so damaged that both port engines threatened to stop through lack of petrol. Eventually, the flight engineer improvised repairs that enabled the Stirling to limp home.

On the night of 30/31 January 1943, Stirlings of No 7 Squadron and Halifaxes of No 35 Squadron were jointly responsible for the operational début of the new radar aid to navigation and target identification known as *H2S* when they used the device to help them groundmark Hamburg for main force heavies of 1 and 5 Groups. In the next *H2S* attack, three nights later, a No 7 Squadron *H2S* Stirling was shot down in Holland by a German fighter and the enemy managed to capture some of the 'hush-hush' radar equipment and start to probe its secrets.

Rising losses, helped by its limited ceiling, resulted in the Stirling being supplanted by the Lancaster in Bomber Command as soon as the supply position allowed, but meanwhile, from late 1943, the Stirling was allotted only the less difficult targets including the flying bomb sites which the Germans were building in northern France. Simultaneously it was relegated extensively to mine-laying in enemy waters and supply-dropping to the Resistance movement in France. Even these missions could be extremely hazardous at times, and much effort was made during 1943 to perfect techniques of mine-laying from higher altitudes, not only to help reduce casualties from night fighters, anti-aircraft guns and flak ships but also to outwit the enemy's methods of assessing the numbers and positions of mines laid. Eventually special mines were produced in which the parachutes and packing material protecting their delicate mechanism had been sufficiently improved to allow them to be dropped from 12,000-15,000ft. Then a Pathfinder technique was evolved, so that when necessary a high concentration of mines could be achieved by the use of sea or sky markers accurately placed with the aid of *H2S* . High-level mine-laying finally became an accomplished fact on the night of 30/31 December 1943 when three Stirling IIIs of No 149 Squadron from Lakenheath made the first operational trial. Three aircraft were despatched and despite accurate heavy flak they all successfully laid their mines off Bordeaux from 12,000ft.

Stirlings of the main force last flew as bombers on 8 September 1944, when No 149 Squadron bombed Le Havre, but No 199 Squadron based at North Creake in Norfolk, which had been transferred to 100 (Bomber Support) Group in May of that year, continued to fly Stirlings until mid-March 1945, its 'spoof' duties sometimes including diversionary bombing attacks as well as radio and radar jamming. For this special role its Stirling IIIs were equipped with various electronic countermeasures devices such as *Mandrel* which countered German *Freya* early warning radar, and were readily distinguished at close quarters by the profusion of aerials projecting from the undersides of their fuselages. In all, Stirlings operating with Bomber Command flew a total of 18,440 operational sorties on bombing, mining and other duties, dropped 27,821 tons of bombs and laid a large number of mines in enemy waters. Aircraft losses, from all causes, totalled 769, of which 606 were classified 'missing'.

Two pilots of Bomber Command Stirlings each gained Britain's highest military award for valour, the Victoria Cross. Both awards were posthumous and the first to be gazetted went to Flt Sgt R. H. Middleton, an

Australian, for his outstanding gallantry during a raid on Turin on the night of 28/29 November 1942. Whilst en route to Turin, his Stirling I BF372 'H-Harry' of No 149 Squadron had great difficulty in climbing to 12,000ft to cross the Alps. Middleton was therefore forced to use excess petrol to achieve height, with the result that there was barely enough left for the return journey. Eventually the Stirling reached Turin, and while making its third run over the city at only 2,000ft so as to positively identify the target, the aircraft was hit by light flak, the first strike tearing a large hole in the port wing, making it difficult to maintain lateral control. A shell then burst in the cockpit and a splinter tore into the side of Middleton's face destroying his right eye and exposing the bone over the other eye. He was probably wounded also in the body and legs. He lost consciousness for a time and his co-pilot, Flt Sgt L. A. Hyder, although himself wounded in the head and both legs and bleeding profusely, eventually managed to regain control of the Stirling at 800ft, climb to 1,500ft and release the bombs.

When Middleton regained consciousness he ordered Hyder back to the rest station to receive first aid and for four hours the Stirling staggered and wallowed towards home, far behind the main bomber stream. Middleton was cut off by the pain from normal communication with his crew and could see very little, and crossing the French coast at 6,000ft the Stirling was again hit by light flak. When at length the English coast appeared ahead, petrol for only five minutes' flying remained in the tanks, so Middleton ordered his comrades to bale out while he flew along the coast, after which he intended to head out to sea. Five of the crew landed in England, but the front gunner and the flight engineer, who had remained to assist their gallant captain as long as possible, jumped too late and were both drowned. Middleton himself stayed with the Stirling which, at approximately 03.10hrs on 29 November, crashed in the sea. His body was washed ashore off Shakespeare Cliff, Dover, on 1 February 1943, and he was buried with full military honours. His posthumous VC was gazetted on 15 January 1943.

The other Stirling VC went to Flt Sgt A. L. Aaron for his part in another attack on Turin, on the night of 12/13 August 1943. His Stirling III EF452 'O-Oboe' of No 218 Squadron from Downham Market, Norfolk, was approaching the target when it was fired on by the rear gunner of another Stirling who mistook it for an enemy fighter. The time was 01.20hrs and the unknown gunner's burst raked 'O-Oboe' from starboard to port wing and back again. Three engines were hit, the windscreen shattered, the front and rear turrets put out of action and the elevator control damaged, causing the aircraft to become unstable and

Above: There was little rest for Stirlings seconded from front-line service to crew-training duties, as exemplified by this study of BIs of No 1651 Conversion Unit.

Above right: The first Stirling Mk IV, all of which were built at Belfast. This model was produced both as a glider tug, with nose and dorsal turrets deleted (and sometimes tail turret, too) and a towing yoke installed round the tail; and as a paratroop transport with a glazed cupola replacing the rear turret and a large paratroop exit hatch under the rear fuselage aft of the bomb bay.

Right: The Stirling V was an unarmed transport with lengthened and hinged nose, and a large cargo door in the starboard side of the rear fuselage. It had a crew of five, as opposed to the bomber models' six or seven, and could accommodate 40 passengers or alternative loads. The last were not withdrawn from RAF service until 1946.

difficult to control. The navigator was killed — a bullet passed clean through his heart — and other crew members were wounded. Aaron was critically wounded; his jaw was smashed, part of his face torn away, a lung perforated and his right arm broken. As he slumped forward over the control column the Stirling dived several thousand feet. Control was regained by the flight engineer at just below 4,000ft and the bomb aimer, who had been at the bombsight in the nose at the time of the attack, then took over from him.

Aaron was moved amidships where he could receive first aid, but not before he had scratched a message with his left hand on the back of the dead navigator's log urging the bomb aimer to head for England. The bomb aimer, after taking stock of the situation, decided to head south towards the nearest British-occupied territory — Sicily. Eventually, 'O-Oboe' crossed the Italian coast at Spezia, where the bomb load was jettisoned (although, unbeknown to the crew, one bomb hung up), and, in reply to an emergency signal, received a message from Bone airfield on the North African coast to head for Bone rather than attempt a landing in Sicily. Fuel was perilously low by the time Bone was finally reached, and Aaron, back in his seat at the controls, summoned his failing strength

to attempt the hazardous task of landing the damaged Stirling in the darkness.

Because a main runway had been blocked by a crashed Wellington bomber it was decided to make a belly landing alongside the runway. Aaron made two attempts but on each occasion he instinctively recognised that something was wrong and ordered the bomb aimer to open the throttles to enable him to go round again. However, on the third attempt the bomb aimer wisely disregarded his captain's wishes due to the desperately low fuel state and got the aircraft down safely himself. The time was 06.00hrs on Friday the 13th, and nine hours later Aaron succumbed to his wounds. He was buried with full military honours in Bone cemetery and his VC was gazetted on 5 November 1943.

Specialised glider tug and transport variants of the Stirling were produced during the latter half of the war, and although these are outside the scope of this article it can be mentioned that the Mk IV Airborne Forces derivative of the BIII played a vital part in the airborne operations in Normandy and Holland in 1944 and during the crossing of the Rhine in March 1945. As well as towing gliders and dropping paratroops, they dropped food, arms and ammunition to agents and partisans in enemy-occupied territory, bombed tactical targets and carried fuel to the fighter and light bomber squadrons of the 2nd Tactical Air Force based on the Continent. Early in 1945 the unarmed Mk V transport entered service, and this model soldiered on until 1946 when, with the run-down of Transport Command, it was retired from service.

Altogether 2,381 Stirlings were built, including 11 destroyed during German air raids before they had flown. More than half of the total output originated from Northern Ireland — Shorts' main plant at Queen's Island (Belfast) and its satellite factories at Aldergrove and Meghaberry — the remainder came from Shorts' Rochester (Kent) plant, the South Marston (Wilts) shadow factory and Austin Motors at Longbridge (Birmingham). Production ended when the final Mk V (PK186), from Queen's Island, was flown at Sydenhan on 8 December 1945.

Buffaloes in the Desert

LARRY MILBERRY

Since 1956 Canada has participated in United Nations' peace-keeping operations in the Middle East. Two communications flights, Nos 114 and 115, originally provided air transport throughout the region from their bases at Capodicino, Italy, and El Arish in the northern Sinai. The Canadian units had as their basic equipment a collection of DHC Otters, Fairchild C-119s, Dakotas and Caribous employed on logistics and communications duties during the 1950s and 1960s.

When hostilities erupted between the Arabs and Israelis in 1967 and again in 1973, the United Nations' presence was withdrawn on each occasion, but re-established once the bullets stopped flying. After the 1973 war, a new Canadian unit, No 116 Air Transport Unit (ATU) was formed for Middle East service. On 2 January 1974 two DHC Buffaloes, the nucleus of the ATU, took off from CFB Trenton on a ferry flight to Cairo. At the end of a short residence there, the unit relocated to its present base near Ismailia on the Suez Canal, south of Port Said. The base is shared by various ground and air elements of the United Nations (in mid-1978 the contributing member countries included Australia, Poland, Finland, Sweden and Malaysia in addition to Canada) as well as by Egyptian military units.

Regular flying operations conducted by the UN-assigned aircraft included those of the Buffaloes, a Malaysian Skyvan and four Australian UH-1 Hueys. A Jerusalem-based Balair F27 Friendship was a frequent visitor, and there was one arrival scheduled each week by Canadian Forces and RAAF Hercules; support for the Canadian team at Ismailia is also provided by a weekly CF Boeing 707 service by No 437 Squadron which operates into Cairo.

The personnel of No 116 ATU comprises 47 men and women each serving a six-month tour; there are nine officers, including seven pilots, an engineering officer, and an adjutant. The unit's strength is drawn from bases across Canada, principally from the Canadian Forces squadrons which operate the Buffalo — Nos 442 (CFB Comox), 424 (CFB Trenton) and 413 (CFB Summerside). The airfield at Ismailia has a 4,000ft runway aligned 14/32 and is equipped basically for daytime VFR (visual flight rules) operations, though night flying occasionally takes place when the runway is lighted by flarepots. The control tower is operated by the Egyptian Air Force whose controllers demonstrate an acceptable standard of spoken English.

When not flying, the Buffaloes of No 116 ATU are usually parked on the ramp along with the Skyvan,

Above left: The UN communications unit base at Ismailia with the two No 116 ATU Buffaloes outside the crew shack, and the Skyvan seen in the background.

Above: Close-up view of the Malaysian registered Skyvan, 9M-AQG, which was based at Ismailia during the Author's visit. / *All photos in this article are by the Author*

while the Hueys use the hangar. Routine servicing of the fixed wing aircraft is conducted outside, with heavier maintenance undertaken inside as required. Near the ramp are a small air movements unit building and crew shack, while alongside is No 116's living accommodation — tents, hard-wall barracks and a large trailer equipped as a washroom. Also in the complex is the unit's well known social and recreation centre, 'The Barn'. In the camp proper there are many other Canadian facilities — messes, swimming pools, the Base Exchange, etc.

In fulfilling its role of air transport support to the United Nations Emergency Force, No 116 ATU flies passengers, mail and freight on scheduled routes five days a week. The locations served from Ismailia are Tel Aviv, Jerusalem, Damascus, RAF Akrotiri in Cyprus, Ras Sudr and Abu Rudis: Ras Sudr is a UN observation post on the Gulf of Suez while Abu Rudis, also on the Gulf, is the Finnish Battalion HQ for the Southern Buffer Zone. The ATU's utilisation of the two Buffaloes amounts to about 150hr/month, of which 130hr consists of UN-related tasks and 20hr of training sorties.

A typical series of tasks were scheduled for No 116 ATU during the author's visit to Ismailia on 21-22 April 1978. Preparations for the first flight of the day began early on the 21st with the unit's technicians readying Buffalo '452'. Then the flight crew arrived: Lt-Col Doug Veale, Aircraft Commander; Capt Ian Stenberg, First Officer; M/Cpl Gary Dentremont, Flight Engineer; and M/Cpl Claude Caron, Loadmaster. The aircraft was loaded with 1,033lb baggage and freight and 278lb mail plus 26 passengers — Canadians, Poles and Finns bound for their postings. Designated as UN Flight 57, the Buffalo was airborne at 08.35hrs and set course for Damascus, 357 miles distant.

Flight 57 flew north at 3,000ft, holding carefully to the 10km wide corridor reserved for UN aircraft between Ismailia and Port Said, and established at cruise speed of 220 knots. Below lay the desert and, stretching to the horizon, the Suez Canal. Also visible were the scars of war — bomb and shell craters, razed towns, a knocked-out tank atop an abandoned fortification and the wreck of a Mirage fighter. Passing to the east of Port Said the aircraft crossed the coast and flew over the great fleet of freighters and tankers moored offshore awaiting passage southbound through the canal. Out over the Mediterranean Sea, Flight 57 climbed to 9,000ft, its next assigned altitude. Two course changes had already been executed by the onboard Omega navigation system and 12 more waypoints lay ahead before arrival at Damascus.

Before long Cyprus and the Lebanese coast showed clearly on the radar scope and the Buffalo swung east. It climbed again, this time to clear the Lebanese coastal highlands. Beirut International Airport passed below, and the scenery changed from the green of the sea to snowy peaks, parched and rocky slopes, and the verdant Litani valley. As the flight entered Syrian air

space near the town of Diemas a fighter strip appeared. Near the runway could be seen patterns of small pads in tight circles — surface-to-air missile (SAM) sites. On 9 August 1974 Canadian Forces' Buffalo '461' under command of Capt Gary Foster was brought down by a salvo of three SAMs fired from Diemas. All nine Canadians aboard lost their lives in this bizarre incident.

Flight 57 arrived at Damascus at 10.20hrs. The author's initial impression, as first-time visitor to this modern airport was of the volume of FOD ('foreign object damage' material, ie loose objects on the ground which could cause damage to aircraft powerplants or airframes) blowing everywhere! The Buffalo joined two civil Boeing 727's and a Twin Otter on the ramp where most of its passengers deplaned. Heavy defences were evident at the airport and included troops, tanks, anti-aircraft emplacements, and hardened quick reaction facilities for use by fighter aircraft.

While the pilots planned the next flight and obtained their clearances, 20 passengers, mostly Poles bound for Ismailia, boarded the aircraft. Flight 57 was airborne again at 11.25hrs en route for Tel Aviv, 260 miles away. The Ben Gurion International Airport inbound pattern was intersected at 12.48hrs and within a few minutes the Buffalo was shutting down at the main terminal. A new set of weather reports and flight clearances were obtained, after which the crew (accompanied by the author) spent some time roaming through the airport's big duty free area. The Polish passengers, being *persona non grata* in Israel, had to sit it out aboard the Buffalo.

An additional passenger boarded the aircraft, and at 13.33hrs Flight 57 took off for Ismailia, a 397-mile leg. The final sector was extra long as Egypt requires UN aircraft to fly well out over the Mediterranean beyond the range of Israeli fighters which it fears could one day use UN aircraft as shadows while actually conducting surprise raids! During the return flight the crew used the time to review ditching drills, these including procedures for jettisoning the cargo should a real emergency occur. On that occasion, a total power failure or other major problem would have allowed a nine-minute glide time to splashdown from the height we were flying, and it was concluded that every effort would be made to jettison cargo which would pose a hazard to passengers upon ditching.

After an uneventful return to Ismailia, the No 116 ATU technicians again took over the Buffalo, while the crew headed for 'The Barn' and a well deserved beer.

The following day '452' operated as UN Flight 41: Ismailia-Akrotiri-Jerusalem-Akrotiri-Ismailia, again with Lt-Col Veale in command. The First Officer was Lt-Col Jim Forrestal, just arrived from No 442 Squadron at CFB Comox to take over as the new unit CO. As this was Jim's initial flight in the Middle East, his day was one long briefing — on flight planning, corridors, en-route landmarks, emergency procedures, etc. As with most trips, ILS (instrument landing system) approaches were made at each destination. This is a routine with No 116 ATU, and designed to increase flying proficiency in view of the marginal number of hours allotted to training each month. Jerusalem airport was quiet during the Buffalo's

Left: A pre-flight inspection of Buffalo '452' before a mission from Ismailia.

Right: The passengers walking out to the aircraft as the loading of baggage, freight and mail is completed from a UN truck via the Buffalo's rear fuselage ramp.

Below: The co-pilot uses a quiet moment to write-up some essential paperwork.

stopover, with only a domestic airline Viscount and a Saudi-registered Falcon (on loan to the UN) in evidence. RAF Akrotiri in Cyprus, on the other hand, was busy with Canberras, Buccaneers, Vulcans, Whirlwinds and a VC-10 all in evidence.

On its homeward leg Flight 41 was informed that the weather had deteriorated at Ismailia. A sandstorm had blown up and an earlier mission, UN Flight 68 involving an F27, had already been forced to divert to Cairo. The question for Flight 41 then became whether to push on or to divert to Tel Aviv for an overnight stop. In the knowledge that afternoon sandstorms tend to abate as the day cools it was decided to proceed as planned and to try a landing at Ismailia. On arrival there the winds were still high, and gusting across the runway at up to 40 knots the maximum crosswind which the Buffalo can accept. An initial approach was abandoned as the runway was lost to sight. The Buffalo pilots found this condition similar to the effect of blowing snow in the Canadian Arctic where they routinely operate. A second attempt was successful, the Buffalo plunking down solidly after a blustery approach.

More prevalent during winter and spring, the sandstorms are just one of several unique features encountered by '116' in its day to day operations. When the wind reaches 30 knots or so, the sand rises to 10,000-15,000ft, and visibility remains restricted for some time even after the wind subsides owing to the lengthy period over which sand particles are suspended in the air. Winds of 10-20 knots produce a haze which is almost always present in this region. Airborne sand can create IFR (instrument flight rules)

115452

Above: Flight 57's passengers en-route Damascus-Ismailia during one of the Author's flights with No 116 ATU.

Left: The ground crew getting on top of a servicing task with one of the Buffaloes at Ismailia.

conditions where minutes earlier VFR (visual flight rules) had prevailed. It also causes technical problems by increasing turbine blade wear in the Buffaloes' T64 engines; and adding noticeably to basic aircraft weight.

Besides the vicissitudes of nature, No 116 ATU faces other difficulties. Although they are served by an expert maintenance crew, it is sometimes difficult to keep the Buffaloes flying: a major difficulty is the availability of spare parts. Those on hand are limited and include a lone spare engine and prop. Ismailia is at the extreme end of a very long resupply pipeline and obtaining spares via the UN administrative channels is time consuming. During April 1978, Buffalo '460' was grounded for lack of a spare oil return line. The part had been ordered direct from CFB Trenton, not through the UN, but failed to arrive on the weekly Hercules service. Two ATU technicians were then sent to Baden Soellingen in Germany on the Hercules in the hope of getting the part made up at the 1 Canadian Air Group base there. The word from Baden, however, was that it could not be done. Fortunately the part arrived in Germany on a CF Boeing 707 before the technicians departed, and they were able to take it back to Ismailia with them. With the part in hand, '460' was back in the air in short order after spending 11 days collecing sand on the tarmac.

Another challenge for No 116 ATU has been the ever changing political and military situation. This has heightened the mood of daily operations and kept the unit sharper than ever. An example has been the contingency flight plan for use en-route to Damascus when Israeli fighters were operating up the coast towards Beirut. On such days, the Buffaloes have had to take a long detour northward around Beirut. Procedures like this are followed precisely.

Other special problems for the unit's personnel have included the adjustment to extremes of temperature, which range from 5°C to 50°C; living in no-frills accommodation with sand getting into everything; going without lights and hot water when the generators are out of action; parasite infested water; sharing a tent with a variety of local creepy-crawlies; and, finally, the separation from their families at home. Everyone has had to cultivate a locally relevant life style which encompasses 'popping' the weekly anti-malaria pills and keeping current with cholera shots.

Nonetheless, No 116 ATU is a contented unit. Hard work and inconveniences are offset by encouraging aspects of life — 'The Barn', the messes, Canadian films and radio, camaraderie with the other flying units, trips to Cairo, and 'R & R' (rest & recreation trips) to Aqaba where the scuba diving is superb. A local goodbye ceremony holds special meaning to '116' — the *Ma El Salaam*. This event bids farewell to those completing their tours and ensures an evening of great conviviality, with feasting, toasting and entertainment. Thus do Buffaloes survive in the desert.

Founding the Jet Fighter era at Glosters

JAMES GOULDING

Below: The first prototype of the Gloster F9/40, serial number DG202/G — the 'G' signifying that the secret aircraft was to be provided with an armed guard. The prototype was painted with Dark Green and Ocean Grey (MAP shade) upper surfaces, all yellow undersides, and a sky blue rear fuselage band.
/ All photos with this article supplied by the Author

One day in September 1941, having completed a course in draughtsmanship, I joined Gloster Aircraft Ltd as that lowest form of animal life in the technical departments — a junior draughtsman. A callow youth stumbling on the bottom rung of the ladder I may have been, but to me life was wonderful and it was thrilling to be, at last, actually working on real aeroplanes — even if only on paper and concerned with minor parts at that.

Before joining the company vague rumours had reached my ears about strange aeroplanes being designed at Glosters and a stressman friend of mine had irresponsibly mentioned a peculiar small monoplane that had trundled around Brockworth airfield; it did not have a propeller and produced a shrill whining sound. My initial job in the drawing office on that first morning at Glosters was to carry out a modification to an existing drawing, and my excitement can be imagined when the drawing proved to be a large side-view of an aeroplane called the F9/40. Immediate features of the big monoplane were the pilot seated up in the nose, six 20mm cannon, a big central fuel tank, the tailplane set high on the fin and an unusual undercarriage arrangement with a wheel unit in the nose. Other drawings around the office showed fat, but shapely nacelles — some without any obvious form of propulsion, although there were others which had spinners for security. I was so excited about what could be seen and asked so many questions that years later I found out that people suspected me of being a spy! I don't think even James Bond, however, could have started his activities as such a raw individual.

When I joined the company the technical offices were installed in a farm at Bishops Cleeve, a tiny village a few miles from Cheltenham. From the outside, apart from several Nissen huts in the orchard, there was nothing unusual about the place. To the casual observer it looked like any other farm, complete with pigs and other livestock. The drawing offices were housed in the Nissen huts, but Mr W. G. Carter, Gloster's great chief designer, and his close associates were accommodated in the main, old farmhouse together with some other departments. The girls of the tracing office (who made permanent ink tracings of the pencil drawings prepared by the draughtsmen) where installed in a private house down in the village, more because of a lack of room at the farm than the necessity to keep them separated from the draughtsmen and strategically-placed haystacks! While at the temporary residence of the farm a splendid new complex of buildings was being built at Bentham, about six miles from Gloucester, amidst beautiful country beneath Crickley Hill, near Birdlip. The new unit was to house all the drawing offices, other technical departments such as the stress office, the lofting office, project office, technical publications and spares department, and other important units. There were the drawing office stores, the drawings library and tracing office. A large hangar housed the aircraft mock-ups and experimental department, wherein all the new prototypes were to be built or assembled. Beside the hangar was a hardstanding for engine running and gun butts. And, very important, there was a large canteen. The whole unit was surrounded by barbed wire fencing.

The time came when Bentham was ready and we prepared to leave the farm, but just when the move was about to be made a German reconnaissance aircraft dropped flares over the district. Fearing a follow-up attack on Bentham our re-location was delayed, but eventually we moved in. For about a fortnight we felt naked and exposed because all the new buildings and concrete were bright and could be seen for miles. The day came, however, when an army of painters arrived and, with the aid of nets, transformed the big buildings into a small village set amid countryside, using the true Bentham village church alongside the Gloster unit to improve the effect. The unavoidable, but essential, water tower was cleverly built in the middle of a group of elm trees within the unit.

Meanwhile, at the Gloster factory, components of the F9/40s were built and the exciting day came when the first piece of real aeroplane arrived at Bentham on a 'Queen Mary' trailer. This component, a rear fuselage, was put into the experimental department hangar and was destined to be part of the first prototype, DG202. Having become familiar with the shape of the new fighter on paper, it was a wonderful moment to see part of it in three-dimensional metal form.

The initial order for the Gloster F9/40 twin-engined jet fighter had been for 12 prototypes, numbered DG202-213. This was an unusually large number, but it was obvious that not only was the type to be developed into a fully operational fighter, but would also be ideal for test flying the large variety of gas

turbine engines under development, especially with the added safety of a twin-engined layout. In the event the last prototype to fly was DG209; DG210, a second Metro-Vick F2-powered aircraft, was only partly built and the rest of the prototypes were cancelled because production aircraft were by then available. The initial production order was for 20 Mk Is under the name of Gloster 'Thunderbolt', but this was changed to 'Meteor' to avoid confusion with the P-47. While awaiting completion of the big twin-engined fighter, jet propulsion was proving to be a practical and very promising new power source in the successful flights of the Gloster E28/39 single-engined experimental aircraft, which was being flown at Edgehill, near Banbury. Our first chance to see a jet engine running was when the E28 was brought back to Bentham for a change of engine. The little aeroplane was inside the hangar with its jet pipe poking out between the nearly-closed hangar doors. There was an armed guard outside the hangar, and the engine was run to show everyone what it was like — it was said afterwards that several people had fainted in the hangar during the engine run. It is not known if this was true, but the shrill scream of the impeller fan inside the buildiing must have been unbearable. Outside the hangar all that could be seen was the tiny jet pipe projecting through the doors and the shimmer of the hot stream of exhaust gas. The engine was run at less than half throttle, but it did give us a foretaste of the future. The E28 also had a change of wing, the new unit incorporating a revised high-speed aerofoil section in place of the original high-lift type used for early trials. For a long time afterwards the old E28 wing could be seen in the Bentham hangar covered in dust.

One by one further components of DG202 arrived and the F9/40 began to take shape. Eventually the first prototype was complete and sprayed with Dark Green and Ocean Grey on the upper surfaces and overall yellow on the undersides. It carried the Sky band on the rear fuselage, because it was a fighter prototype, and the prototype 'P' marking in yellow aft of the fuselage roundels. Mock-up engines (made mostly of metal parts, but with some wooden items) were initially supplied to Glosters for positioning pipe and wiring 'runs', but soon two working engines arrived for DG202. These engines, however, were not suitable for flight and were for taxying trials only because they were limited to 1,000lb thrust each — quite insufficient power to maintain height if one engine failed. Officially these engines 'were not to leave the ground', but in reality they did for a few feet during high speed taxi runs down the runway.

After preliminary engine tests outside the Bentham experimental hangar the first prototype F9/40 was taken on a 'Queen Mary' to Newmarket Heath, an RAF aerodrome, on 22-June, 1942. Taxi trials began on 10 July with the Chief Test Pilot, Gerry Sayer, at the controls. Gerry had done all of the flying of the E28 up to this time and was, therefore, the only pilot with jet experience in this country.

F9/40 airframe development was at this stage well ahead of the various engines. The Whittle engine production had been placed with Rover Motors, the engines being designated W2Bs. Two W2Bs were to be delivered for proper flight trials by the end of August 1942, but in the event various problems arose in engine production and DG202 had to gather dust while awaiting suitable engines. Meanwhile, de Havilland's big powerful Halford H1 gas turbine was behaving well and a pair of these engines were to be fitted in DG206, the fifth prototype, which had a wider centre section and much bigger nacelles. As these engines seemed likely to become available before W2Bs, DG206 was brought forward in construction. Other F9/40s were also being completed and lay in the hangar awaiting engines.

The summer of 1942 was a frustrating time for Glosters; we had exciting new fighter prototypes but could not fly them. There was uncertainty about what form the production Meteor would take — whether it would be the Mk I with Rover W2Bs, or the Mk II powered by Halford H1s. At this time the Gloster project team was working on a new single H1-powered fighter, the E5/42. This had a low-wing layout, with Vampire-like air intakes, a tail-down undercarriage, four cannon projecting from the nose and a high T-tail. A wooden mock-up was built and some components of a prototype were partially built, and at one stage, due to the problems with the Rover engines, consideration was given to cancelling the Meteor in favour of the E5/42. From drawings and the mock-up it certainly looked an attractive little fighter, but some two years would have been lost in getting a jet fighter into service with the RAF if this course had been followed — and the Vampire would certainly have got into service before the Gloster fighter. Some of the E5/42 experience was built into a later project, the E1/44, which did of course fly, but not until after the end of the war.

With the ground running engines Gerry Sayer had completed all the necessary taxying trials before the first prototype returned to Bentham to await flight engines. During the course of these trials DG202 had shown a willingness to fly and had been lifted off the runway for brief periods, but there was nothing for Gerry to do but await the day when he could take the F9/40 into the air for the first real flight. Meanwhile, he and the other Gloster pilots continued with their routine duties of testing the Typhoons that were pouring out of the Hucclecote factory, some 3,300 of which were built by the company. Gerry was always eager to keep up-to-date with new developments and

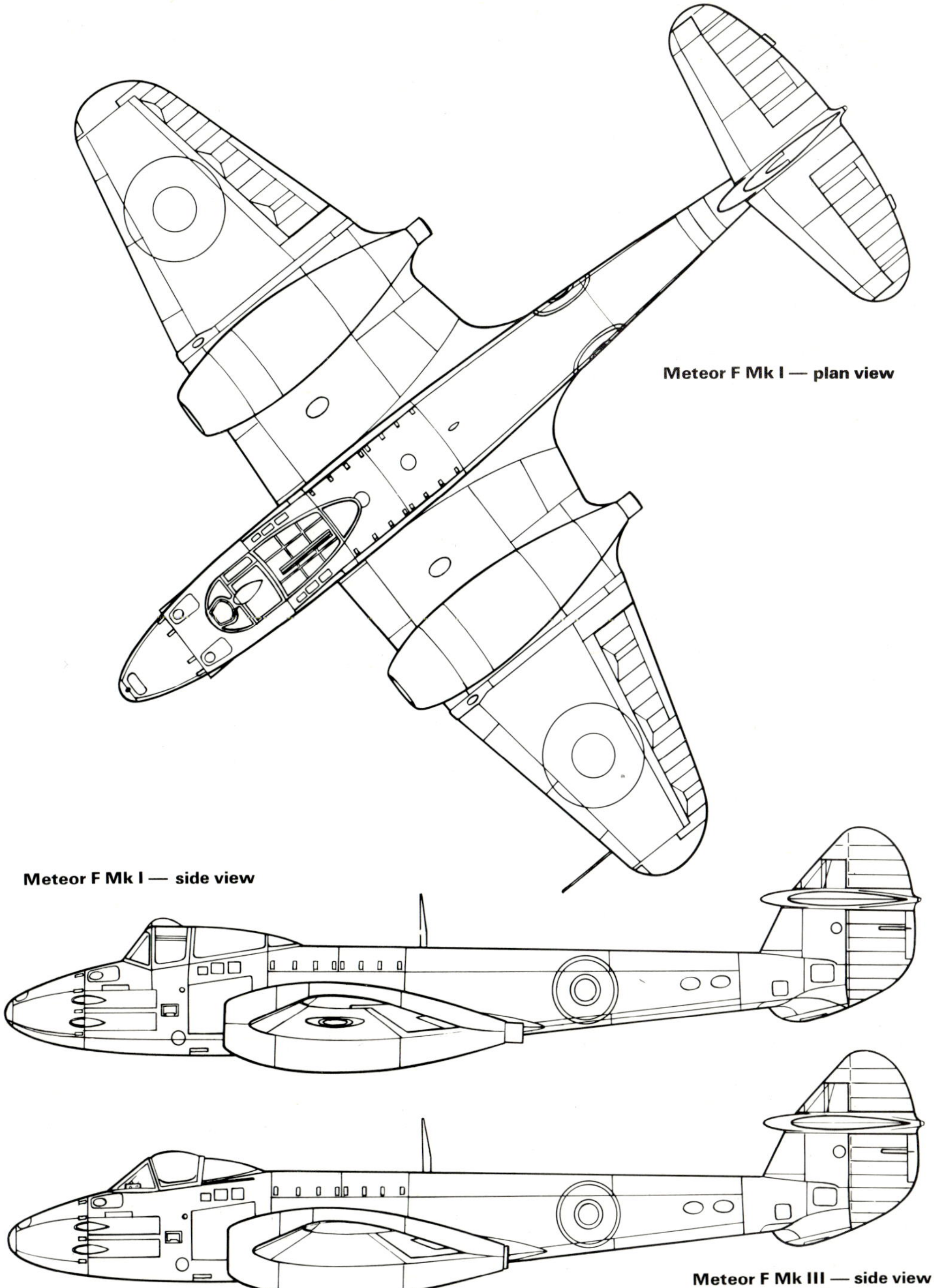

Meteor F Mk I — plan view

Meteor F Mk I — side view

Meteor F Mk III — side view
Drawings by the Author

he visited RAF Acklington to test a Typhoon fitted with a gyro gunsight. On 21 October 1942 he and another Typhoon pilot took-off for a flight over the North Sea — neither of them returned. The news that he was missing had a stunning effect on everyone at Bentham and I can well remember the gloom and despondent silence that spread throughout the offices. His death, presumably in a mid-air collision, posed more problems for the Meteor programme but fortunately his deputy, Michael Daunt, had been kept well informed and the task of flying the first F9/40 (to be DG206) was to be his as the new chief test pilot.

Early in the New Year (1943) DG206 was completed, with Halford H1 engines cleared for flight. Throughout the days that followed we heard for the first time the strange, shrill whine that was to become such a characteristic of DH Halford engines, as DG206 underwent a prolonged series of engine tests outside the experimental department. It was during one of these engine runs that a new phenomenon became apparent, the engine intake suction effect. Michael Daunt was walking near an intake when he was lifted bodily and swept head first into the intake. Mike weighted 14 stone but it took only a matter of seconds for the accident to happen. Fortunately, such was the layout of the compressor fan that it was impossible for any part of his body to make contact with the rapidly revolving blades, and he only suffered shock and severe bruising. After being hauled out of the intake he was said to have remarked, 'why the hell don't you feed the brute'! I saw the intake shortly after the incident and it was considerably buckled.

During the latter part of February 1943, DG206 was taken from Bentham to Cranwell for flight trials and on 5 March it became the first British jet fighter prototype to make a proper flight.

Above: Gloster F9/40, DG206/G, the fifth prototype and fitted with Halford H1 engines, became the first of the type to fly when test pilot Michael Daunt made the maiden flight from Cranwell on 5 March 1943.

Above right: DG204/G, the Metro-Vick F2-powered prototype, seen outside the Experimental Hangar at Bentham. This aircraft was lost in April 1944 when the engines disintegrated during an aerobatic manoeuvre.

By this time the experimental workshop was looking very busy, with a number of F9/40s in various states of assembly and several types of engine, both working and mock-up (although there were far more of the latter) to be seen. DG202 was still there awaiting engines and the similar DG205 was also nearly complete. The hood fairing on DG202 was unique, being 'solid' all-metal and having strange recessed cut-outs for rear vision, as on the Reggiane Re2001 fighter, whereas the rear hood fairing on all subsequent F9/40s and Meteor Is was transparent. The revised type was also fitted to DG206 which was now engaged on flight trials.

A very interesting prototype nearing completion was DG203, powered by two Power Jets Ltd (Whittle's company) W2/500 engines, and armed with the original design complement of six 20mm cannon. This was a devastating punch and I once had the shattering experience of standing near it when all six were fired simultaneously into the butts near the hangar. Eventually, the two lower guns were dispensed with in favour of the standard armament of four cannon with an increased supply of ammunition. Apart from the standardisation on a four-cannon configuration in the RAF, there was a serious problem

with the two lower guns in the Meteor; if a live round jammed, the gun had to be withdrawn from the aircraft through the structure towards the armourer, a very hazardous operation. Incidentally, the mounting structure for the two discarded guns remained within the front fuselage structure of all Meteors, although the gun ports were skinned over.

Following DG206, the next F9/40 to fly was DG205, at first powered by two Rover W2B/26 engines — the powerplant was one of the variety of gas turbine engines under development. DG205 had left Bentham in May and had been taken to Barford St John, a new temporary airfield for the jet programme, where it commenced taxying trials on the 28th, the same day on which DG206 made the first British cross-country flight by a jet aircraft. On this flight it flew from Newmarket Heath to Barford. Up to this time the testing of DG206 had taken place at Cranwell and it was transported to Newmarket by road before being flown to Barford.

It was about this time that the inhabitants of Bentham were given a delightful flying display by John Grierson flying W4041, the first E28/39. We could see the thin smoke trail as the small single-engine jet took off from Brockworth a few miles away and in a short while it was making a series of very low level runs over the Bentham buildings. To many people this was their first sight of a jet-propelled aeroplane and the decision to give this little brief display to the Bentham staff was a good one. It was flown with great verve, borne of the confidence which by now had been built up in this lovely little aeroplane. It certainly didn't look like a delicate, temperamental experiment, but a glimpse into the future of fighter development.

One day during the early summer of 1943 we got our first view of the F9/40 in the air. It was just after lunch when an unfamiliar aircraft sound, rather like an organ note together with a whining noise, heralded the appearance of two F9/40s, DG206 and DG205 (all the F9/40s and E28/39s carried the suffix '/G' after the serial number, denoting the need for a guard on the aircraft in the event of a forced landing), flying together overhead — a most exciting occurrence.

A third F9/40 joined the flight test programme when DG202 at last made its first true flight, this being on 24 July, almost a year since its initial taxying tests. Flown by Michael Daunt, DG202 was powered by W2B/23 engines. Two more of these engines were now also installed in DG205 in place of the W2B/26s. The entire engine development programme had been, up to then, remarkably free from serious problems, but it was around this time that the first engine failure in flight occurred in DG205. The incident was due to a rear bearing failure, but the aircraft was landed without any problems on the power of the 'good' engine.

During July 1943, DG204 was completed; this F9/40 looked markedly different from its relatives. It was powered by two Metro-Vick F2 axial flow turbines, by far the most advanced British engines in design concept, mounted in underslung nacelles. These engines had the same basic layout as used in modern fighter power units, but in 1943 they suffered from many problems. They offered potentially very high thrust, but were much heavier than the Whittle or Halford designs. Just after the war Metropolitan Vickers even produced designs of a development of the F2, which was the world's first fan engine. Installed in DG204 the F2 engines suffered from a major problem — excessively high idling thrust. DG204 began taxying trials at Barford St John on 3 August, but it became obvious that the idling thrust would make

Above: Meteor F Mk I, EE212/G, as flown without the lower rudder and rebound bumper during directional stability trials. / *Imperial War Museum*

Above right: Another attempted 'fix' to overcome the 'snaking' problem on the Meteor Is was tried on EE227, which had the upper fin and rudder removed.

landing on the Barford runway impossible and the engines were therefore removed and returned to Metropolitan Vickers for modification.

This period saw the move of the flight test department from Barford to its new permanent home at Moreton Valence, near Stroud, Glos. Here excellent facilities had been built for the jet programme. There were runways with unobstructed surrounding areas and security was good, the airfield being out in the country. Internal security was also very tight and getting into Moreton was quite a business, with advance notice by phone and then screening on arrival. The flying prototypes were ferried to Moreton by the test pilots, with other F9/40s following by road. It was during this time that Farnborough took over jet engine development flying, leaving Glosters to concentrate on developing the F9/40s into the fully operational Meteor fighter. Some of the F9/40s and the two E28/39s were therefore transferred to Farnborough. DG204 was moved to Moreton Valence from Barford where modified Metro-Vick F2 engines were installed. Some authorities say that DG204 was transferred to Farnborough and made its first flight from there, but I definitely saw it flying over Gloucester on one Saturday morning. It is possible, therefore, that it was flown first of all from Moreton Valence, although equally it might have been flown over to Gloucester from Farnborough for some reason.

Engine development accounted for quite a lot of test flying time during the early days, with engines constantly being replaced, new versions of existing engines arriving for test flying, and mock-up engines being installed to check clearances and pipe runs for new variants. Bentham and Moreton Valence were often littered with odd engines, jet pipes and other components, such as wings, ailerons, elevators, etc.

Flying controls, and ailerons in particular, caused many headaches before satisfactory answers were found. On the F9/40s and Meteor Is 'snaking' (directional instability) was a persistent problem and at first it was wondered if it was due to some inherent defect in twin-jet aeroplanes resulting from the effect of the high-speed exhaust gases upon the tail unit. It was then suspected that the basic formulae for calculating fin area could be incorrect — without the de-stabilising effect of propellers, and that the fin area might have been too large. Consequently some F9/40s were flown without the bottom fin and rebound bumper and one Meteor I was flight tested without the entire upper fin and rudder. This did not improve the situation and it was then thought that possibly, there was too little fin area, and DG208 was flown with increased upper fin area. It was even proposed to add a long fin extension from the tailplane down to the rear fuselage/centre fuselage joint. Again, the results

were negative and other causes had to be sought. At this period it was considered possible that lateral instability might be the cause and the wing-tips were modified with a turned-up angle to give the effect of increased dihedral, but again the 'snaking' persisted. All the F9/40 and Meteor I controls were fabric-covered at this time and this eventually proved to be the cause of the problem — flexing of the ailerons: the provision of a metal covering effected a cure. Concave ailerons were tried, but the optimum type proved to be flat-sided.

The lack of air brakes highlighted a problem peculiar to jet aeroplanes which had not been envisaged with the old 'up and down' engines; because of the lack of propeller drag and overall 'cleanliness' of the new airframes, it was easy to overshoot one's aerodrome. Without airbrakes jet aircraft took a long time to lose speed and it became necessary to shut down the engines in ample time to allow the aircraft to slow down for the landing. The development of suitable airbrakes for the Meteor became a priority. The first versions tried were simple flat plates, but when opened these nearly tore the airframe apart, so perforated types were finally adopted.

The end of July 1943 saw the loss of the first British jet-propelled prototype when W4046, the second E28/39, got into an inverted spin with iced up controls at 37,000ft. The RAE pilot left the E28/39 at 33,000ft, an extremely high altitude without oxygen and in ordinary flying overalls, but he landed safely by parachute.

Soon after the move to Moreton Valence an interesting new jet-propelled aeroplane arrived — a Bell XP-59 Airacomet twin-engined fighter prototype, which was to be exchanged for the first production Meteor F Mk I then nearing completion. I remember walking around this American aircraft and being amazed by its massive size compared to the F9/40s, although dimensionally it was generally similar. It was its bulkiness and thick wings that made it look so much bigger, and the cockpit was much roomier than on the Meteor. It was armed with two 37mm cannon, with only 44 rounds per gun. Two points I well remember were that all the controls were fabric-covered, including the massive trailing edge flaps, and the interior of the Airacomet was painted in yellow chromate primer in contrast to the pale greenish-grey of our F9/40s and Meteors. Its appearance was cumbersome, it seemed too hefty to be powered by the two GEC-Whittle units and its slow-firing cannon (these were later replaced by six 0.5in guns) were not suited to snap-shooting in fighter vs fighter combat. I did see it flying on one occasion and it didn't look very impressive, but the prototype did fly a few months before the F9/40. About the time we had the Airacomet at Moreton I was talking to an American GI, who was sitting next to me on the bus, when an F9/40 flew overhead quite low down. He told me it was 'one of the new American jet planes' and remarked that he was surprised that the British hadn't designed jet aeroplanes of our own! Seething inside, I had to let the remark pass because the F9/40s, Meteors and E28/39 were still top secret. The veil of secrecy was slightly lifted when a local ATC cadet exhibited a model of the Meteor in a tobacconist's shop window in Gloucester, but the police hurriedly

had the balsa model removed from the window and had some words to say to the offending lad!

After being complete for some months DG203 — powered by Power Jets' W2/500 engines of 1,640lb thrust each — was eventually flown for the first time on 9 November 1943, from Moreton Valence. On its intended second flight the compressor fan of one engine distintegrated just before take-off, peppering the nacelle and the hood fairing with metal fragments. Fortunately, Michael Daunt was unhurt but when the aircraft was brought back to Bentham for repair we were amazed to see just how much damage could be done by this type of failure. It looked as if it had been raked by machine-gun fire, with jagged holes through the nacelle engine bay door, the fuselage sides, the hood just behind the pilot's head and other parts of the airframe. While it was being repaired W2/700 engines of 2,000lb thrust were installed in place of the defective engines, and the pilot's cockpit was modified to incorporate a pressure cabin, a design feature always intended for the Meteor. The sealing of all joints and rivets was rather crudely done with black Bostik (which I believe was developed for the purpose). After pressure testing, the cockpit interior was sprayed with Night (black) paint.

The tempo of Meteor development was ever-increasing: components were beginning to pour into the production shops, where impressive lines of fuselages and centre sections began to form. By the end of 1943 the first production Meteor F Mk I, EE210, was complete and on 12 January 1944 it made its first flight. After a series of tests it was dismantled and shipped to America, where it was sent to Muroc, Calif, (now site of Edwards Air Force Base) to commence a series of test flights.

The first flight of another prototype, DG208 took place on 20 January: the aircraft was powered by Rolls-Royce (who had taken over production from Rover) WR1 engines, early versions of the Rolls-Royce Welland. DG208, as mentioned earlier, had an increased fin area to try and cure the 'snaking' problem — the attempted solution was unsuccessful, however.

April 1944 was a bad month for the Gloster jet programme after a comparatively trouble-free series of trials. On the 1st of the month, Sqn Ldr Davie, the brilliant young RAE test pilot who had got out of the second E28/39 was killed in DG204 when the Metro-Vick engines disintegrated during aerobatics — causing the F9/40 to break-up in the air. This was a sad loss of a fine pilot, who would probably have become one of the great postwar test pilots. From Gloster's point of view even worse was to follow on the 27th. John Crosby-Warren, who had built up considerable jet-flight experience and was one of the few such pilots in the world, was flying DG205 when he ran into severe aileron trouble during a high-speed dive. Aileron flutter set-in, tearing away the end-mounted mass-balance weight, and causing the aircraft to roll into the ground at Minchinhampton Common, near Stroud, Glos, at a steep angle and at very high speed. DG205 had done much excellent test work, probably more than any other F9/40 at the time, and it was testing a spring-tab aileron design at

Above: Meteor Mk Is and IIIs of No 616 Squadron, the RAF's first jet fighter unit, which started to receive its new equipment in July 1944. / *Imperial War Museum*

Above left: DG207, the Meteor F Mk II prototype; it was later used by the de Havilland Engine Co as a test-bed for the Goblin engine.

the time of the accident. The gruesome remains of the aircraft were brought back to Bentham and laid out on a workshop floor. The whole airframe had disintegrated into small fragments and even the engine combustion chambers were compressed flat, end on, but there was little sign of fire damage. John Crosby-Warren was to be sadly missed in the test pilots' team and the accident was all the more unfortunate because it was not related to the new form of engine propulsion, except in that the 'clean' jet aeroplanes could achieve very high diving speeds. The aileron failure, probably caused by a spring-tab fracture inducing flutter, could have occurred on any high-speed aeroplane and the tragic accident did not hold up jet propulsion development.

In April DG203 returned to the test programme following its repair, but after a few flights another impeller fan disintegrated — this time in flight, with fragments causing damage to such an extent, particularly to the tail unit, that Michael Daunt prepared to abandon the aircraft (there were no ejection seats in the F9/40s and early Meteors in those days). Eventually he made a skilful 'wheels-up' landing in a field, incidentally a tribute to the handling of the F9/40 and an action which would be quite unthinkable in present day jet fighters. Once more DG203 was out of the test programme for some time.

The loss of three F9/40s from the test schedule was fortunately not such a severe blow as might have been the case earlier. Production Meteor Mk Is were now coming off the Brockworth line in a steady flow, although not yet at a high rate, and they were adding to the overall jet experience. Plans were speeded-up to get the fighter into service as soon as possible. To this end three Mk Is — EE216, EE217 and EE218 — were delivered to Wg Cdr H. J. Wilson's flight to train squadron pilots and conduct high-speed trials. These aircraft, the first jet aeroplanes to enter service with the Royal Air Force, were delivered on 22 June 1944, with EE219 following on 1 July. On 23 July, these four Mk Is, together with EE215, were delivered to No 616 Squadron, which thus became the first operational RAF jet fighter squadron. EE215 was the first Meteor I to have the full cannon armament and was used to test the guns completely in air trials. Later it went to Farnborough to have the first application of reheat to a jet aeroplane, which added 40mph to the top speed. Two other Meteor Is, EE213 and EE214, were delivered to No 616 as non-operational aircraft to complete 150hr of experimental flying and iron out any problems in the process. These aircraft were painted yellow on the under surfaces and were known

Above: The final F9/40 prototype was DG209; powered by Rolls-Royce W2B/37 engines of 2,000lb thrust each, the aircraft was first flown during June 1944.

Centre: The Gloster Meteor F Mk III, and . . .

Below: . . . a close up of the much improved windscreen and hood design adopted in the light of early squadron experience with the F9/40s and Mk Is.

Above: The second production Meteor F Mk I, EE211/G, later used for trials of lengthened engine nacelles. */ Imperial War Museum*

to the squadron pilots as 'yellow bellies'. Seven other Meteor Is were delivered to the squadron during August and September. The Meteors were used operationally against V1 flying bombs, where the fighter's low-altitude top speed of 420mph gave it an advantage over piston-engined fighters whose engines developed maximum power at around 18,000ft.

One problem that arose at this time was the collapse of the Meteor noses while they were firing their guns in high-speed dives. This seemed to have been caused by the combined effects of gun blast and compressibility, and the immediate answer was to double-up on all nose skins until noses with thicker gauge skins could be put into production. Gun jamming proved to be another snag, and it was after such an event that Flg Off Dean in EE216 toppled over a V1 with his wing-tip to score the squadron's first victory.

While No 616 Squadron was becoming operational, the last F9/40, DG209, was completed and flown during June 1944. This prototype was powered by Rolls-Royce W2B/37 engines of 2,000lb thrust. These engines were early examples of the Rolls-Royce Derwent 1 and the thrust obtained was double that available at the time of the original taxi trials of DG202. The Derwent 1 engine was to be the main power unit of the Meteor F Mk III, which was the first major production version of the Gloster jet fighter. The Meteor III incorporated improvements made in the light of early squadron experience and extensive test flying of the F9/40s but perhaps the most important change from the pilot's point of view was the entirely new windscreen and hood design and the introduction of air brakes as standard.

When an Fw190 landed by mistake at RAF Pembrey earlier in the war, it had given an opportunity for new design features to be examined by the aircraft industry. Gloster's design draughtsmen used the 190's laminated, toughened glass windscreen design in the Meteor III, and it was a great improvement in both protection and forward vision over the old Meteor I windscreen.

Such did the pilots' confidence in the aircraft and engines develop, that it was not unusual to see a Meteor up on a test flight half roll into a dive and come sweeping across the Bentham buildings at a little over roof-top height, scattering the rooks from the elm trees. We greatly appreciated these little displays, which made one realise that jet propulsion was no longer a tentative scientific experiment but one which would become the normal power source for many classes of aircraft in the future. During the closing stages of the war, thrust ratings in the region of 5,000lb were becoming a reality in engines under development, like the DH Halford Ghost and Rolls-Royce Nene, and much higher thrusts were promised in the Armstrong Siddeley Sapphire and Rolls-Royce AJ65 Avon.

George Carter was never in any doubt about the future of jet propulsion and told a friend and myself that in due course piston engines would be replaced by gas turbines in almost all types of aircraft. However, another very famous, but conservative chief designer, who occasionally visited Glosters, thought the whole idea of jet propulsion was a lot of nonsense. Although he at first had a deep suspicion about such a new-fangled idea he subsequently went on to design one of the world's classic jet fighters.

The first Meteor F Mk III, EE230, made its maiden flight during September 1944, and this version went into service with No 616 Squadron in December 1944, augmenting the existing Mk Is. The Mk IIIs were used operationally on the continent, usually attacking ground targets with their four cannon.

EE211, the second production Mk I was used for tests of a new nacelle designed to alleviate buffet due to compressibility. The new shape retained the same diameter but was much longer to improve the finesse ratio. EE211 was first flown with only the forward part of the nacelle lengthened, but eventually the entire nacelle was longer and proportionally slimmer. The result was a total success and the last 15 Mk IIIs incorporated the lengthened nacelles. Only the smaller jet pipes and intercooler outlets on the engine bay doors distinguished these Mk IIIs from the much more potent Rolls-Royce Derwent V-engined early production Meteor F Mk IVs with full span wings.

The Meteor never met the Messerschmitt Me262 in combat, but much has been written denigrating the Gloster fighter in comparison — which is, I feel, unfair. It is true that the Meteor Mk Is and Mk IIIs were not as fast as the Me262, but the Gloster design was aerodynamically 'clean' and possessed an excellent high-speed wing section. Unlike the Me262, which was somewhat underpowered, the Meteor was a tractable aeroplane to which any ordinary fighter pilot could convert. Like some other German wartime projects the Me262 used technology that was more advanced than was necessary for what could be achieved on the existing engine power. With the complication of a thin, moderately-swept wing, which served to increase the handling problems for the average pilot, the Me262 attained a safe Mach number of 0.83, whereas the orthodox Meteor was eventually cleared for safe operation up to Mach 0.82. The true benefit of a swept wing is realised in transonic flight, and then with fairly sharply swept wings. A high speed trials Me262, with a small redesigned blister canopy, achieved a speed of 621mph and an almost standard Meteor Mk IV with better external finish, reached a timed speed of 616mph. It could be argued that the use of a slightly swept wing, with its attendant problems of increased weight and the need for low-speed devices, was an unnecessary aerodynamic luxury.

Right: Meteor F Mk III, EE457, fitted with long engine nacelles. Note also the intake mesh guards, known at Glosters as 'anti-Daunt guards' after the discoverer of the requirement (the story is recounted on page 60).

Front-Line T-6 Texans

JERRY SCUTTS

Above: Seen at Seoul in October 1952 is a line up of 6147th TCG Texans, four of which are fitted with spray equipment under each wing. The distinctive cowling and tail trim is believed to have been a means of Flight identification, although the colours are unconfirmed.

Above right: Mustangs of the 18th Fighter Bomber Wing armed with bombs and rockets about to taxy out for an airfield strike in July 1951.

Right: Flying day and night, B-26 Invaders did sterling work in Korea, those of the 3rd Bomb Wing operating throughout the conflict. Bearing the white tail tip of the 90th Bomb Squadron, aircraft 'W' is s/n 44-35881.
/ All photos in this article — USAF, via the Author

When the armies of North Korea stormed across the 38th Parallel in the early hours of Sunday 25 June 1950 to precipitate a full scale war, the United Nations forces opposing them were critically under strength. Nowhere was this weakness more evident than in airpower, which was to be the deciding factor during the 37-month conflict. Pared down drastically by postwar policies, the US Air Force (which was to bear the brunt of operations) hastily marshalled what forces were at its disposal in the Far East to meet the threat.

Fortunately, the rapid destruction of the obsolete aircraft types with which the North Korean Air Force was equipped at the start of the war enabled UN ground-attack sorties to go ahead unmolested, but there was a most urgent need to ensure that available aircraft were used to the best possible effect and, to that end, Lts James A. Bryant and Frank G. Mitchell undertook the first tactical air control operation of the war, on 9 July. Flying a borrowed Army L-17, these men successfully controlled 20 flights of F-80s. That mission was the first of many which were to lead to the formation of one of the most important air organisations in Korea, the 6147th Tactical Control Squadron (Airborne).

Tactical operations, essential to retaining a UN presence in Korea, were roughly divided into three requirements: containing an enemy advance; inflicting the maximum losses of men and material once it had been stopped or at best slowed up; and interdicting supply lines in order to prevent supplies reaching the front lines.

When the war broke out, the nearest FEAF (Far East Air Force) air base to Korea was Itazuki in Japan, 350 miles from the front. This meant that the sole available jet type, the F-80 Shooting Star, could spend only about 20min over the target, even when carrying two 165gal wing tanks. Nevertheless, jets had the advantage of being able to get into and out of the target areas quicker than piston-engined types, and their use was considered essential. Thus a programme of fitting locally-made 265gal wing tanks to the F-80s was put in hand, the so-called Misawa tanks boosting range to some 350 miles depending on load carried. In

FF-037
FF-515
FF-476

W

the face of increased drag, not to mention popped rivets and cracked wing-tips, the F-80s kept up the sortie rate in company with B-26s, F-51 Mustangs and F-82 Twin Mustang night fighters, some of which were on standby virtually round the clock.

It came to be realised that the short time allowed for ground attacks resulted in only 25% of sorties despatched actually finding their targets in the early days of the war: the need for positive location of the enemy in the mountainous terrain and fluid battle lines became paramount.

Initially, the pilots and observers that formed the nucleus of the 6147th flew under Army, rather than Air Force jurisdiction, the parent unit being the 24th Infantry Division. A number of such flights were made from Taejon before the arrival of Maj Merrill H. Carlton on 11 July 1950.

Carlton took command of the unit and two days later it moved to airfield K-2 at Teagu in the south, sharing what facilities there were with F-51-equipped 51st Fighter Squadron (Provisional). On 15 July the callsigns from which the squadron would soon take its nickname were allocated, the spotter aircraft being identified as 'Mosquito How', 'Mosquito Able' and so on. The generic word Mosquito stuck.

While the first TAC (or FAC — Forward Air Control) missions were solely for the location of targets and direction of fighter bombers by radio, the reconnaissance role — necessary to complete an up to the minute picture of enemy movement and disposition — was soon added. Other important tasks were progressively allocated to the 6147th and these included leaflet dropping, airborne briefing of VIPs and correspondents, and the location of refugees and guerilla groups. Above all, flexibility was the squadron's byword.

The month of July saw the number of missions completed since the outbreak of hostilities rise to 269, and two aircraft were listed as missing. The official unit designation was bestowed on 1 August, and towards the end of that month the 6147th TCS(A) could count 55 pilots on the roster — and another two crews lost.

The aircraft mainly used was the T-6F version of the North American Texan, 27 of which were on hand by 1 September. In an effort to extend the T-6's basic combat range of 629 miles, four machines were fitted with 58gal belly tanks in September, extending endurance to six hours or 1,000 miles.

In transit again on 4 October, the 6147th went to K-14, Kimpo, the most modern air base in Korea at that time. But the rapidly changing ground situation forced another re-location that month, to K-16, Seoul. By late October the Texans were flying from K-24, Pyongyang East, and they were back at K-16 before the end of the month. Such a nomadic existence brought deprivations, both in personal comfort for the crews and maintenance people, and in shortages of

aircraft spares. Any T-6 that suffered a heavy landing and was deemed unfit for flying was immediately cannibalised to keep others in the air. Useful items discarded by the units that happened to share a base with the 6147th were also pressed into service where possible.

Establishing something of a record by flying on all but two days until the end of 1950, the 6147th soon standardised on the T-6, although other types were used occasionally. It cannot be said that the T-6 was the absolute ideal for the exacting — and highly dangerous — work that was the lot of the squadron, but it had a number of attractive qualities that made it the obvious choice over other available types. It was adaptable and had a good maintenance record (each aircraft used by the 6147th averaged 5.65 flying hr/day in 1950) and its flying characteristics were right. Considering the unit's sortie rate (7,174 effective sorties in 2,000 combat hours by 22 January 1951 for the loss of 23 aircraft) and the increasing important of its role to the conduct of the air war, Korean service was an outstanding tribute to the design of the T-6. To do its job successfully, the unit had to have aircraft flying from first light to dusk, every day, often using airstrips that were not of the solid, flat variety because of the need to be as near to the front as possible. The Texan could take off in 700ft, whereas the F-51 and F-80, for example, needed 1,800ft and 3,090ft respectively. With its excellent loiter time and slow flying characteristics coupled with an acceptable top speed of 215mph, the Texan soon endeared itself to the crews. One drawback was the poor downward view from the rear seat due to the low wing, a problem not encountered with types such as the L-5 and L-19, but, as implied, the T-6 was able to offset that disadvantage with a far greater 'survivability' over the lighter machines.

This picture: The first jet type to see action in Korea, the F-80 Shooting Star initially suffered from limited range when forced to operate from bases in Japan. Flying from Korean bases, however, the jets could use their enhanced loiter time to great advantage on ground attack sorties. This typical scene shows aircraft of the 80th FBS/8th FBW heading north with two 1,000lb bombs apiece.

Equipped, therefore, with a reliable and sturdy aircraft, the 6147th was to write a new chapter in the history of the USAF's Tactical Air Control System (TACS). Such a system had remained in being after the end of World War II, but had not previously needed the air component found to be essential in Korea. When Army air observation flights were begun from Taejon, headquarters of the Joint Operations Centre (JOC) at 8th Army HQ, they were as a result of requests made by Army field commanders. Calls for air support were then passed to the Air Force's combat operations section, which controlled the aircraft earmarked for close support work. But an efficient close air support request network could not be established due to lack of equipment and personnel and because the Army was without a signals unit in the theatre.

Following attempts to bridge the gap by using air liaison officers attached to Army units, and relaying messages via land line or radio, both of which failed due to equipment breakdown and the distances involved, the emergency procedure became standard practice. This involved sending requests for air support to divisional tactical air control parties or directly to the JOC by the 'Mosquitoes', using ARC-3 radio.

Although this latter technique had the slight drawback of further cluttering well utilised radio channels, it was employed until early 1952, when the Army updated its communications equipment in Korea. Obviously a large number of target sightings

Above: As the first Commonwealth air unit to go into action in Korea, No 77 Squadron RAAF used Mustangs to devastating effect before a change of equipment. Meteor 8s of No 77 Squadron are seen at Kimpo in September 1951 with, from left, A77-982, -189 and -373 identified.

Above left: A scene that apart from the aircraft markings, could have been photographed a decade earlier than May 1951. It shows two 6147th TCG 'Mosquito' Texans undergoing maintenance prior to a strike control sortie, while a 315th Air Division C-47 takes-off.

Left: The type of tableau enacted time and again when the job has to be done despite the facilities to hand.

continued to originate with the airborne FAC rather than Army units, enabling air strikes to be carried out before an enemy move could become a threat to friendly ground forces.

Actual strike planning and execution was also problematical; in the first instance, a daily 'frag order' detailing resources was written up every morning. It gave information on all available aircraft in the theatre and divided them into allocations for each type of mission — close support, reconnaissance, air defence and so on. Preplanned missions were noted along with the targets each aircraft was to attack. For immediate close support missions, the frag order merely stated that aircraft were to come on duty and be scrambled by JOC order to the base commander.

While most of the fighter bombers were based in Japan during the first critical months of the war, unreliable communications meant that it became routine to simply scramble one mission every 15min. All the time the enemy was attacking in strength, this system worked well enough but it was uneconomical if the ground situation changed rapidly. Then, the air control pilot could easily find himself with dozens of fighter bombers orbiting over a peaceful area and none where they were needed; others might be unable to reach a critical area due to fuel shortage. Thus by gradually being able to monitor the entire front, the 'Mosquitoes' could assess with remarkable accuracy where and what kind of air support was required.

Tactical air control capability was further improved by the introduction of 'Mosquito Mellow'. This was the callsign of a Texan orbiting at 10-13,000ft, between ground control and the front line 'Mosquitoes', whose function was to send fighter bombers from one sector to another quickly and keep up a running commentary of enemy movements. The 'Mellow' duty was passed to C-47s in January 1951, the larger aircraft being able to carry seven radio operators. It was the task of the senior controller to divert incoming fighters from a quiet sector to an active one, often by splitting four-flight sorties into two of two aircraft each.

As target identification for the fighter pilots became the most important task of the 'Mosquitoes', control of attacks fell into five main categories: air traffic

control; ordnance selection; target discrimination; damage assessment and strike aircraft evaluation.

As it had become impossible to regulate the rate at which aircraft (often of both jet and piston-engined type) arrived over the target area, the 'Mosquitoes' had to quickly marshal their forces with minimum delay. Jets, with their short duration, had to be particularly rapidly deployed. Aircraft usually arrived in flights of four, to be divided into two sections by the controller, who instructed one pair to remain at high altitude while the second element carried out the required strike. The attacking machines used all weapons apart from cannon and machine guns and changed places with the two flying high cover. Finally, all four would strafe the target before turning for home. If a target was considered particularly tough, several flights of fighter bombers could be on hand at once so that those carrying the most effective ordnance were able to attack first. If there was little difference in the loads carried by available aircraft, then their ability to stay in the target area was the primary consideration. Consequently, the FAC would 'stack' each type at various altitudes, those at the top acting as cover for those performing strikes. In the event, no UN aircraft ever came under enemy air attack whilst actually engaged in ground attack in Korea, but the practice continued to be followed. With the best endurance of all types, US Marine Corps F4U Corsairs took the highest position in the stack, then F-51s and F-80s, F-82s and F-84s in descending order.

When passing his request to 'Mosquito Mellow', the T-6 pilot would state his preference for weapons, depending on the target; obviously he did not always get what he selected, but the ideal was a combination of 50cal machine gun, 20mm cannon, light 3in rockets and fragmentation bombs for 'soft' targets such as buildings, vehicles (including ox-carts), troops on roads, bivouac areas, barges, mortar positions, small villages, automatic weapons and combustible stores or storage dumps. More substantial munitions, 5in rockets and 500lb General Purpose bombs, were used against tanks, bridges, railway tunnels, artillery and anti-aircraft guns and positions. Large, well contructed bridges and tunnels required 1,000lb bombs. Napalm was used against all targets except railway tracks, as in most instances even a near miss would stop a tank or knock out an artillery piece. It was also the weapon most feared by enemy ground forces.

In the early days of the war, accurate pinpointing of targets for fighter bomber pilots was one of the most demanding tasks faced by the 'Mosquitoes'. Various methods were tried to perfect the technique. At first, the procedure was to describe the target over the radio, giving fullest possible details of landmarks and their location in relation to it. These reference points included roads, geographical features and panels — coloured cloths laid on the ground or worn by friendly troops and visible to the fighter pilot. 'Talking the pilot in' was soon found to be unworkable, because the strike aircraft frequently failed to find the target and the already crowded radio channels were not reliable enough. Following the makeshift expedient of waggling the wings when his radio went out during a strike, one 'Mosquito' pilot led the way to improved visual target marking. Diving passes were made, or the Texans flew wing-to-wing with the attacking fighter bomber towards the target. The latter method was

Above: Rocket-laden Texans of the 6147th Squadron taxi out for another mission as part of 'the most dangerous aerial activity of the Korean war'.

Above left: With some 130 missions recorded, Republic F-84E-25 Thunderjet of the 49th Wing stands ready to sortie again during the last weeks of the war. *Linda Charlotte* was almost certainly the wing commander's aircraft.

effective but dangerous, as it not only called for precision flying, but exposed two aircraft to ground fire instead of one.

Early in 1951 actual target marking, as distinct from target description, was introduced by the T-6 crews. Both smoke-emitting and white phosphorus grenades were dropped by hand, out of the rear cockpit. Some success was achieved, but the scheme had three main drawbacks — grenades were difficult to aim; only about 30% of them continued to smoke after hitting the ground; and they frequently exploded prematurely, severely shaking the aircraft and crew. Flares proved little more effective than grenades and the time-honoured use of bursting artillery shells was only successful if there were good air-to-ground communications, and, of course, if the target was in range of the guns which it frequently was not.

In actual fact, the best method of target marking was initiated the month the war started, when Maj Carlton recommended that the T-6s be equipped to carry small size rockets with high explosive heads. First supplies of rockets were received in mid-September and crews immediately set about learning how best to employ them to locate targets. The munition itself was a 2.36in marking rocket with a white phosphorus head, which occasionally proved to be an effective weapon in its own right. This was shown the very first time that rockets were used in anger by FAC aircraft when the third missile fired disabled a self-propelled gun. The standard rocket load was 12, carried on 'trees' of three each on four wing racks. As soon as crews were proficient in the use of rockets, the weapons rapidly became standard equipment on the T-6s; during the first month of combat alone, up to 30 a day were being expended.

When a target was deemed to have been destroyed or badly damaged by an air strike, the 'Mosquito' pilot decided whether further attacks were required or what other targets there were, and released aircraft low on fuel or which had used all their ordnance. Additional aircraft would be called via 'Mosquito Mellow' as required.

Damage assessment needed good photographic coverage for an accurate appraisal and although aerial photography was not part of the 6147th's role originally, cameras were carried from January 1951. By that time there were enough K-20 and K-24 cameras, photo labs and interpretation equipment in Korea to begin operations, the observer undertaking the task from his rear seat. The results were disappointing: as photographs could only be taken with the aircraft held in a steep bank, they were always at an angle and invariably had important details obscured by shadows. Only vertical frames were

considered of any value for accurate evaluation and, later, vertically-mounted aerial cameras were fitted into the T-6s in the rear cockpit aft of the wing.

It did not take the enemy long to realise the importance of the little trainers flown by the 6147th in directing the devastating air strikes to which he was continually subjected, and accordingly every effort was made to shoot them down. Even by the second month of the war, the Communists had increased their 20mm anti-aircraft capability by deploying 40mm AA guns. Rare was the day when a 'Mosquito' Texan landed unscathed after a sortie; things got so bad by December 1951 that Fifth Air Force began to fly flak-suppression missions in order to ensure the safety of FAC aircraft. Despite the hostile conditions, however, none of the T-6s were fitted with armament other than that intended for marking purposes, although personal side-arms were normally carried by crews. Tactics changed little in order to increase self-protection, although the 'Mosquitoes' could sometimes reduce the odds a bit. One way was to get down low — very low. During visual reconnaissance runs, 50ft became the standard altitude but on 24 October 1950 a T-6 followed a set of tank tracks, keeping them in sight from a mere 10ft. Five dug-in tanks were located as the prize for this hectic run and the vehicles were duly destroyed by fighter bombers. There were times when 'Mosquito' aircraft actually 'captured' enemy troops and vehicles by forcing them to flee into the hands of friendly forces by repeated low passes. Nevertheless Communist groundfire gradually forced the 'Mosquitoes' higher. From 1,200-1,500ft at the beginning of the war, the typical reconnaissance and control altitude was 6,000ft in 1953. Such a height was understandably useless for bomb damage assessment, close visual reconnaissance and marking, so the trainers continued to run the gauntlet of fire at lower levels.

Above: Sharkmouthed F-51 Mustangs of the 12th FBS/18th FBW during a break in operations in September 1950.

Above right: A T-6 being refuelled at a typically primitive Korean airstrip during the autumn of 1950.

Right: Sabres were latecomers to ground attack operations as their forte was air combat. Last to convert was the 8th FBW, which flew a number of F-86 ground strikes. On 18 June 1953, a bare month before the armistice, one of the Wing's aircraft is seen being loaded with 1,000lb bombs.

Discussions took place on replacing the T-6 with something more suited to the hostile environment of Korea, Carlton himself favouring a modified F4U Corsair. Others thought the F-51 could do the job, but nothing came of the ideas. The Texan stayed and before the end of the fighting the squadron had received 59 T-6Fs rebuilt by Temco specially for liaison work, designated LT-6G, the number being made up by some Navy SNJ-6s.

Fifty missions was the normal aircrew tour with the unit that was acknowledged to have had 'the most dangerous of any aviation activity in Korea'. Having completed a tour, an individual could rotate out for a non-combat assignment in Japan, or be transferred to

the operational fighter or bomber squadron of his choice. Alternatively, a number of individual pilots and observers elected to fly a further tour with the 6147th. The composition of the T-6 crew was usually a USAF pilot and an Army or Navy observer. Army personnel began to be carried within a month of the start of operations owing mainly to a shortage of Air Force pilots, but most observers had piloting experience. The majority were selected because they had been light aircraft pilots in World War II and had seen combat. This had many advantages, not least of which was that observers quickly became familiar with Air Force tactics and fighter operations. Secondly it gave the crews the safety factor of a second pilot in the aircraft.

By the end of the Korean war on 27 June 1953, 352,023 ground-attack sorties had been carried out by Far East Air Force fighter bombers for the loss of about 2,000 aircraft. Most of the strikes had been directed by TAC 'Mosquitoes' of the single unit that had proved a new theory in air warfare during its brief existence. The 6147th TCS was given group status on 18 March 1951, when Carlton, then a Lt-Col, handed over command to Lt-Col Timothy F. O'Keefe. Instrumental in enabling UN forces to stay in Korea during the dark days of 1950, the unit was soon forgotten. It was ironic that the USAF had to 're-invent' the FAC role for service in Vietnam using one of the very aircraft that had been rejected by the 6147th, the L-19 (0-1 by the 1960s) Bird Dog!

Representative aircraft (all LT-6Gs) of the 6147th Tactical Control Squadron/Group, Korea 1950-1953: 49-3545/LTA-545, 49-3566/LTA-566, 49-3571/LTA-571, 49-3583/LTA-583, 49-3584/LTA-584, 49-3591/LTA-591.

Into the Second Half-century of the Shuttleworth Collection

DAVID OGILVY

This picture: The scene at Old Warden aerodrome during the flying display held on 24 September 1978 to mark the 50th anniversary of the Shuttleworth Collection. Some of the vintage and veteran vehicles which took part on that festive occasion are seen as the Collection's Spitfire VC makes a fast run across the airfield. / *Martin Horseman*

Right: Gleaming in the sunshine of an autumn morning, the Bristol F2B Fighter's superlative condition belies its veteran years. / *Martin Horseman*

D
8096
D8096

K
3215
8096

Above: The DH60X Hermes Moth was the first aeroplane acquired by Richard Shuttleworth in 1931, and it has lived at Old Warden ever since. It is an exceptionally pleasant aeroplane to fly for the pure pleasure of flying. / *Air Portraits*

Left: The Avro Tutor K3215 has been with the Collection for some 20 years and prior to its temporary (one hopes) grounding in late-1978, it was the only remaining airworthy example in the world. / *Jonathan Bingham*

The Shuttleworth Collection is very fortunate to have a solid base as a result of its founder's action in preserving early aeroplanes at a time when other people threw them away. Today, raptures would abound within the British Aircraft Preservation Council if someone discovered aircraft dating from before World War I, yet in the 1930s Richard Shuttleworth quietly acquired the 1909 Bleriot, 1910 Deperdussin and 1912 Blackburn without which the later (and naturally more recently dated) acquisitions would mean so much less. It would be quite impossible now to set up a complete range covering the development of the flying machine from the earliest pioneer days.

With this background the Collection has developed over a period of half-a-century and the original aim that everything should work has been kept fully alive; nearly all the aeroplanes fly and many of the road vehicles are driven, with more specimens of each constantly passing through the works restoration programme. Although Old Warden is known mainly for the aircraft (for these provide the unique element), the first acquisition was a motor car — an 1898 Panhard Levassor which had quite a history to its name.

Richard Shuttleworth obtained his first aeroplane in 1931; this was a nearly-new DH60 Moth G-EBWD that had been built in 1928 and which he used for what, today, we would call commuting between Brooklands (where he had a workshop and his motor racing interests) and Old Warden. Shortly after obtaining 'WD he removed the original 85hp ADC Cirrus engine and replaced it with a Hermes of 105hp, which produced a correspondingly sparkling performance that bettered both the climb and speed of the more familiar Gipsy Moth. Today, still with this engine aboard, 'WD can claim to have been based on one aerodrome for longer than any aeroplane in aviation history; and it has flown little over 600 hours in its 50 years!

Richard Shuttleworth's aeronautical interests were diversified to cover most of general aviation, although that American term had not seen daylight at the time; his Warden Aviation and Engineering Company (which still exists) carried out charter flights and aircraft overhauls and modifications; also he was a Director of the Comper Aircraft Co, in which capacity he flew a Swift to India on a sales demonstration tour.

By the outbreak of war in 1939, Old Warden was the home of many ageing aeroplanes; in addition to the Bleriot, Deperdussin and Blackburn already mentioned, the 1916 Sopwith Pup (converted into a two-seater Dove on the production line and re-converted to a Pup at Old Warden), Desoutter G-AAPZ and the little ANEC II G-EBJO were part of the scene, although at the time the last of these was privately owned and became Collection property considerably later. Both the ANEC and the

Dessoutter are stored now, but are scheduled for eventual restoration to flying health.

An attractive little rotary-engined Hanriot biplane of 1917 was a regular flier in the late 1930s, but unfortunately this was sold to the other side of the Atlantic for a peanut figure. Another ex-Shuttleworth aeroplane that went into private hands in the 1950s was the Spartan Arrow G-ABWP, but fortunately this has remained on the UK register and has flown again in recent times.

Wartime activities were interesting and varied; with the historic aeroplanes and road vehicles stored wherever space could be found to house them, the only pre-1939 hangar (the present No 1, nearest to the entrance gate) was turned over to work on lighter

Right: The Miles Magister, although in service in considerable numbers into the late-1950s, is one of only two airworthy specimens in the world. The aircraft, P6382 — seen here with the Author at the controls, recently underwent an extensive re-restoration programme including the fitting of the wings from G-AKUA. / *Martin Horseman*

Below: The SE5A, F904, seen here taxying in after a flying demonstration, was restored at RAE Farnborough, but is owned by the Shuttleworth Collection and spends most of its time at Old Warden. The aircraft now has a direct-drive Wolseley Viper V-8 engine in place of the Hispano-Suiza formerly fitted. / *Martin Horseman*

types of aircraft then in Service use. This hangar, soon to be joined by No 2, became a form of assembly line for machines that had been dismantled to receive technical attention at two workshops in the centre of Biggleswade. There is pictorial evidence to prove that Proctors were the sole line occupants at one time, but Harvards and Magisters were fairly regular inmates; even odd examples of impressed civil types such as the Cygnet and Falcon passed through the shops.

In early postwar years, when the aircraft industry comprised a large number of relatively small firms, the Collection was maintained in relatively low key, largely through covenanted donations from some of these organisations; often a historic type that had been retained by its makers would be handed-over for safe keeping, supported by an annual sum towards its maintenance. But such luxury was not built to last; the reshaping of the aviation industry brought to an end most chances of financial help, so other ways were sought to provide the essential finance for the future of the Collection.

This apparent misfortune proved to be the shock that was needed, for only then was Old Warden officially opened to the public. In 1966 the first 'Open Days' were held, when a few hundred people would arrive to stand behind hurriedly-erected temporary fencing to watch three or four of the aeroplanes take to the air. Since then increased public interest has enabled the entire operation to progress through a steady expansion programme. The aerodrome itself has been extended three times, one such improvement involving the Royal Engineers in re-routing a brook as a training exercise.

Today there are six hangars, with various workshops and more than enough exhibits to fill them. There are 28 complete aeroplanes on daily display and at present four aircraft are in various stages of major repair or restoration. In addition to those being tended in the shops at Old Warden, a Sea Hurricane 1 is being rebuilt at Staverton, a Spitfire PRXI and Anson 19 at Duxford and a new Sopwith Triplane is being built from original drawings — and will be fitted with an original Clerget rotary engine — in Yorkshire.

Two of the biggest tasks being tackled at Old Warden are also two of the most interesting projects to have been started. The full story of the famous 1934 DH88 Comet G-ACSS *Grosvenor House* warrants a book of its own, but suffice here to mention that

Below: Another famous WWI biplane fighter kept in immaculate condition by the Shuttleworth Collection is the Bristol F2B Fighter, D8096. / *Martin Horseman*

Above: The Hawker Hind, retrieved from Afghanistan on an overland journey of 6,000 miles, is making marked progress towards completion. This view of the aircraft in the workshops dates from late-October 1978. / *J. E. Hoad*

technical support has come forward from many quarters; Hants and Sussex Aviation have generously overhauled the Gipsy Queen II engines, Hawker-Siddeley Dynamics (as they were) have prepared the variable-pitch propellers, which previously were fitted to Proctors, and British Airways apprentices have produced the engine bearers. Quiet, but very necessary background support has been provided throughout by the Hawker Siddeley Hatfield base, where tasks ranging from stressing to design and construction of the undercarriage retraction mechanism have been performed.

All the airframe structural work has been carried out by the craftsmen at Old Warden and this side of the operation is virtually complete; but anyone who has restored anything will know the dangers of allowing such a situation to minimise the extent of — or the time needed for — the work ahead. A flight date is impossible to forecast, for a few small missing items — such as rubber washers of a non-standard size — can build several months into the total time taken. Everyone is optimistic, though, that G-ACSS will be aeronautically active long before its demi-centenary celebrations fall due in 1984.

A very different aeroplane is the Hawker Hind that was retrieved several years ago from Afghanistan. For a considerable time no skilled manpower could be spared to put the project on course, but recently, progress has been very marked and the aircraft is taking recognisable shape. The Kestrel engine has been overhauled, the radiator (exchanged with that from the Hart in the RAF Museum) and oil cooler have been cleared, a Palmer brake system has been acquired and most parts are coming together again. As the world's only original specimen of the famous Hawker operational-type military biplane range that is ever to fly again, the Hind has a strong following and there is no doubt that it will be in heavy demand at displays. Although a target completion date could be almost as inaccurate as one for the Comet, it is quite possible that the Hind may be the first to fly.

How does it all work? The Collection sits under the administrative umbrella of the Richard Ormonde Shuttleworth Remembrance Trust, which as an educational charity covers also the Shuttleworth Agricultural College, most of Old Warden village and several farms, with a ground coverage in the region of 6,000 acres. The Board as a whole, therefore, has many things to consider other than aeroplanes, so an Aerodrome Committee, with four Trustees and four others, deals with aviation policy and a smaller Executive Committee meets on a monthly basis to keep near to the regular pulse.

Those who attend Flying Days only may well be excused for thinking that nothing else happens, but the

Above: The Supermarine Spitfire VC is the most authenic example of the type still flying today. The only Spitfire still with a three-bladed propeller, AR501 is finished in the markings of No 310 (Czech) Squadron, with which it served at RAF Duxford in 1942. / *Air Portraits*

Centre: For many years the 1912 Blackburn, the oldest genuine original British aeroplane remaining airworthy anywhere in the world, was restricted to straight hops along the aerodrome, but recently it has been 'allowed out' into the circuit when conditions are fully favourable. / *Air Portraits*

Below left: The Bristol Boxkite, a reproduction of a 1910 design made for the film *Those Magnificent Men in their Flying Machines*, is one of the biggest crowd-pullers at Old Warden, but it is the most difficult to fly of all the Collection's aeroplanes. / *Air Portraits*

Collection has ties in many directions as an aerodrome operator, owner and operator of a largish fleet of mixed aircraft types, a transport museum that is open on seven days each week, an education and research centre to which queries come from all parts of the globe and a base for many facets of general aviation. This calls for a range of people with varying skills and abilities; covering aircraft and vehicle restoration and maintenance, the shop, the library, accounts, works and bricks, promotion, publicity and overall administration, the total workforce has been contained at only 26 people and eight of these are engaged on a part-time basis. Not surprisingly, therefore, the workloads can become quite severe; these apply not only on the technical front, where the results appear as proof of what has gone before, but also on the administrative side where the promotion and organisation of at least 10 main flying displays and numerous other events (there were 26 in 1978) can easily pass without notice. In practice, preparation, production and circulation of publicity material alone occupies the major part of the three darkest winter months. Although the type of activity varies with the seasons, there is no slack time; perhaps the situation is comparable with the age-old fallacy that a Sunday is the only day on which a parson works!

What future lies ahead? Clearly a collection such as this cannot tread water for long. However, rapid expansion would do more harm than good, for a main aim must be to retain the irreplaceable timelessness that sets the scene. With no fewer than eight historic aeroplanes in various stages of preparation for display — and for which static exhibition/hangarage space must be provided — any attempt at acquiring further aircraft just because they are getting old could lead to serious disruption and overloading of the system. So an element of consolidation is currently in play. Already several marginally historic machines have been refused on the basis that it could be preferable for them to go to organisations able to devote early attention, whereas any fresh item obtained now might need to wait several years before being fed into the work programme. Despite that, though, anyone with a potentially restorable Hawker Fury biplane or, perhaps, a DH9a, need not fear a rebuff for offering it to the Collection! Similarly, a welcome awaits the person who rolls-up with an Armstrong-Siddeley Lynx engine that will enable the grounded 1931 Avro Tutor to have daylight under its wheels again . . .

Right: A happy conjunction of both the vehicular and aeronautical interests of the Shuttleworth Collection as the Avro 504K trainer warms up after receiving the attention of the 1916 vintage Ford model T-mounted Hucks starter, seen pulling away at the left of the picture.
/ Martin Horseman

The Vought-Sikorsky
SB2U Vindicator

KENNETH E. WIXEY

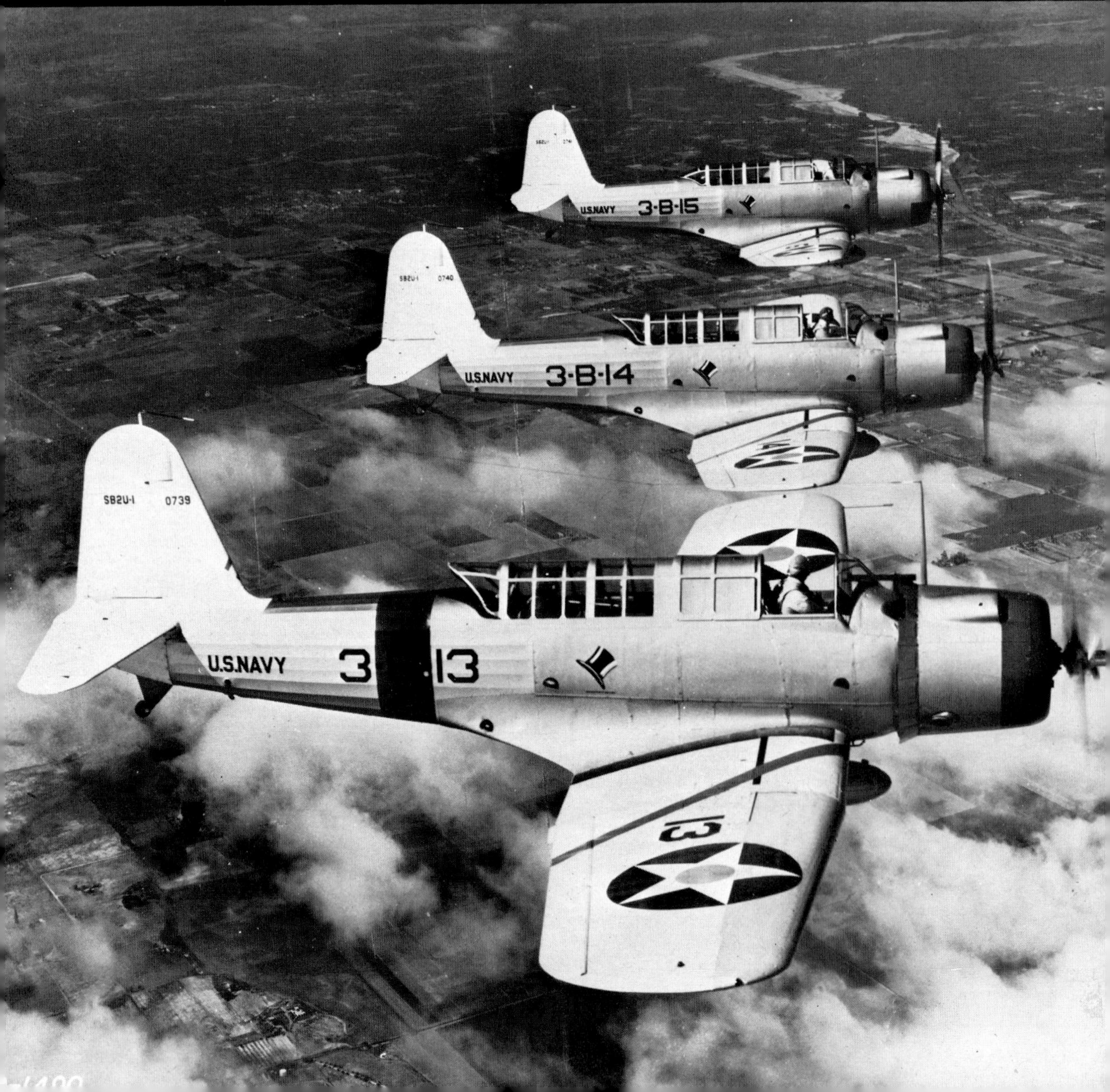

Above: Fresh off the production line, 10 Vought SB2U-1 Vindicators are lined up awaiting delivery to the US Navy. */ All photos with this article are from the archives of United Technologies Corp, via the Author*

Left: Another line-up, this time airborne and featuring a trio of the scout/dive bombers after entry into US Navy squadron service — the aircraft are from VB-3, 'The High Hats'.

Right: A good underside view of a Vindicator during its landing approach, and showing the wheel wells and flaps.

Following the classic biplane scout-bombers employed by the US Navy during the early and middle 1930s, there appeared a new generation of two-seat monoplanes intended to operate in a similar scout/dive-bomber role. The monoplanes were typified by having a low-wing configuration, radial engine, retractable undercarriage and a two-man crew sitting beneath a lengthy 'glasshouse' cockpit canopy. Representative of the aircraft in this category was the SB2U-1, -2 and -3 Vindicator series produced by Vought-Sikorsky, a part of the United Aircraft Corporation.

The prototype XSB2U-1 was ordered by the US Navy from Vought on 11 October 1934, and made its first flight on 4 January 1936. It was subsequently flown to Anacostia Naval Air Station in April the same year for Navy trials.

It is interesting to note that, while at Anacostia, the XSB2U-1 was competing with a new biplane scout-bomber, the XSB3U-1, also produced by Vought in the Chance-Vought Division. Unlike the US Army Air Corps, the US Navy was more reluctant to admit to the idea of monoplanes being more suitable than the established biplane layout, and four months after ordering the XSB2U-1, placed an order for a new biplane scout-bomber as a safeguard should the XSB2U-1 monoplane not live up to its expectations. The XSB3U-1 biplane was in fact based on a previous Vought design, the SBU-1, then serving with US Navy units. The main difference was in the fitting of a retractable undercarriage which folded backwards, the SBU-1 having a fixed landing gear.

The Anacostia trials proved, however, the superiority of the XSB2U-1 monoplane and while work on the XSB3U-1 biplane was cancelled, a production order for 54 aircraft was placed by the Navy on 26 October 1936, the SB2U-1 thus becoming the first monoplane scout/dive-bomber to serve operationally with the US Navy. It was also the first carrier-based monoplane to be equipped with a folding wing mechanism for ease of stowage aboard aircraft-carriers.

Designed by R. B. Beisel, the SB2U-1 (Vought Model V-156), was powered by the Pratt & Whitney SB4-G-R-1535-96 Twin Wasp Junior air-cooled radial engine and was of all-metal structure with a mixed

Right: Resplendent in its special paint scheme, the Vought V-156 export model of the Vindicator was displayed at the French Aviation Exhibition in 1938, where it was the subject of keen interest.

Below: A distinguished visitor gets a close-up inspection of the V-156 at the Exhibition — Thomas F. Hamilton, founder of the Hamilton Standard Co, points out some details of the aircraft's wing folding mechanism to President Le Brun of France, standing on his right.

metal and fabric covering. The fully retractable undercarriage main wheels folded rearwards through 90° to lie flush in underwing wheel wells, the tail-wheel being fixed. The two-man crew, pilot and observer/gunner, sat in tandem in an enclosed cockpit covered by a long 'glasshouse' type canopy. The SB2U-1's armament comprised one fixed forward-firing 0.30in machine-gun and one flexible 0.30in gun in the rear cockpit and the bomb load could be up to 1,500lb.

Deliveries of the SB2U-1s began on 20 December 1937, first machines going to US Navy Squadron VB-3 (the 'High Hats'). The following month the Navy ordered 58 SB2U-2s, these having the same engines but differing from the earlier machines in having an increase in the gross weight due to new equipment being installed. The SB2U-2s were delivered during the second half of 1938 and went to a number of US Navy carrier based units.

On 25 September 1939, the US Navy placed an order for 57 SB2U-3s, these being the last variants of the type ordered for the Navy. They differed in having the Pratt & Whitney R-1535-02 engine, increased fuel capacity and provision for the carriage of long-range tanks on ferry flights. The 0.30in guns were also replaced by guns of 0.50in calibre both fore and aft while the crew were given increased armour protection, the whole resulting in a higher operating weight.

The SB2U-1s and SB2U-2s embarked aboard carriers of the US Fleet and by 1940 were operating with VB-2 (USS *Lexington*), VB-3 (USS *Saratoga*), VB-4, VS-41 and VS-42 (USS *Ranger*) and VS-71 and VS-72 (USS *Wasp*). The majority of SB2U-3s went to US Marine Corps squadrons, initially equipping VMSB-131 and VMSB-231.

Although by 1942, many of the SB2Us had been relegated to secondary duties and training, a number of SB2U-3s were still operating with US Marine Corps units in the Pacific conflict and saw action during the Battle of Midway.

Meanwhile, reverting to 1938, Vought had its eye on the export market and that year at the French Aviation Exhibition, a V-156 in a very highly polished and decorative state was put on show. The then President of France, Monsieur LeBrun, together with other French officials, showed much interest in the scout/dive-bomber with the result that an order for 40 V-156Fs (SB2U-1/France) was placed. Deliveries of these machines had commenced to the *Aeronautique Navale* when the Germans overran France in 1940 and the dive-bombers, unprotected by fighters, were an easy prey for the marauding German fighters. Those French Navy V-156Fs that were not destroyed in the fighting fell into enemy hands and though there had never been any known confirmation of the fact, it was reported at the time that several of the American built dive-bombers operated with the Luftwaffe in raids on the English south-east coast!

In the meantime, a further order for another 50 V-156Fs had been placed with Vought by the French government but with the sudden drastic change in the military situation, the order was transferred to Britain, the machines involved then carrying the Vought designation of V-156B1. These aircraft began to arrive in Great Britain early in 1941 and were destined for service with the Royal Navy, the original intention being that they should operate from British carriers, partly replacing the already obsolete Blackburn Skuas.

Although the name Vindicator had been adopted by the US Navy for its SB2Us, the British V-156B1s were given the name Chesapeake and designated the Mk I. These machines differed from the French V-156Fs in having four 0.30in machine-guns in the wings instead of one forward-firing gun. They also had British-type deck-landing arrester equipment and an alternative radio installation. The Royal Navy Chesapeake Is were allotted the British serials AL908-AL957, many of these machines going to RNAS Lee-on-Solent.

Below: One of a batch of V-156B1 Vindicators purchased for the Royal Navy; in Fleet Air Arm service, the aircraft was known as the Chesapeake Mk I.

After being assembled at Burtonwood Aircraft Repair Depot, the first Chesapeakes went to No 728 Squadron, a Fleet Air Arm training unit at Arbroath. On 14 July 1941, 14 Chesapeake Is joined No 811 Squadron, an operational unit based at Lee-on-Solent. In the event, however, the operational career of the Chesapeake in British service was short-lived. The type was found to be unsuitable for operating from escort carriers due to its long take-off run and was subsequently relegated to secondary duties including training, target towing and night fighter practice flights.

Prior to the adoption by the US Navy in 1941 of the grey warpaint camouflage for its aircraft on operations, the SB2Us were usually finished in the more colourful prewar paint schemes typical of most US Navy aircraft. In 1938 the SB2U-1s of VB-3 (the 'High Hats') from the USS *Saratoga*, for example, were finished with silver fuselage and underwing surfaces and chrome yellow upper wing panels. The complete horizontal and vertical tail surfaces were painted white (unit identification colour for the USS *Saratoga*) while the fuselage and tail numbering and letters were painted black. The squadron insignia, also in black, was a tilted top hat situated on the fuselage side below

Below: Another view of Section Five of the US Navy's VB-3 Squadron as they formate in line against an impressive mountain backdrop in the Western US.

Left: In an altogether different setting from that on the facing page, a Vindicator is shown suspended from a hangar roof during the 1939 World's Air Fair in New York.

the centre of the cockpit. The identifying colour for Section 5 of VB-3 was Willow green, the three SB2U-1s in that section being numbers 13 (BuAer No 0739), 14 (BuAer No 0740) and 15 (BuAer No 0741). The section leader's aircraft, number 13, carried the 20in band in Willow green round the rear fuselage in addition to the normal upper wing chevrons, while the front part of the cowling was completely finished in Willow green. The centre letter 'B' of the aircraft and unit fuselage code (3-B-13) was painted in the middle of the fuselage band together with the hypen either side. This left the numerals 3 and 13 on the silver finish each side of the band. The other two aircraft, 14 and 15, had only the top and bottom halves of their front cowlings finished in Willow green. The national insignia of the United States as applied to its aircraft at that time were carried on the upper and lower wing surfaces.

Those machines serving with the Royal Navy were finished in the standard temperate sea scheme camouflage by then in general use. This was a dark slate grey (more commonly known as grey-green, sometimes dark green) and extra dark sea grey upper surfaces with Sky Type S under surfaces, this again being often referred to as Azure blue. An unusual feature of the markings on the British Chesapeakes was the use of 8in RAF type serial numbers, the Royal Navy by then having reduced its serial number size to 4in. Some of the Fleet Air Arm Chesapeakes carried an individual aircraft letter in white behind the fuselage roundel, one example being AL924 with the letter 'K'.

Acknowledgement

The assistance of Mr Harvey H. Lippincott of United Technologies Corp, Hartford, Connecticut, USA, in the preparation of this article is gratefully acknowledged.

Vought-Sikorsky SB2U-1/2 Vindicator (Chesapeake Mk I)

Manufacturer: Vought-Sikorsky Aircraft Division of United Aircraft Corporation, Stratford, Connecticut
Role: Two-seat carrier-borne scout/dive-bomber
Engine: One 750hp Pratt & Whitney SB4-G-R-1535 -96 Twin Wasp Junior air-cooled radial
Span: 42ft
Length: 34ft
Height: 10ft 3in
Wing Area: 305ft^2
Max Speed: 257mph at 11,000ft
Climb Rate: 1,545ft/min
Service Ceiling: 27,400ft
Range: 700 miles at 227mph
Weight: 4,500lb (empty)
6,500lb (normal loaded)
7,278lb (max take-off)
Armament: (SB2U-1) One fixed forward-firing 0.30in machine-gun and one 0.30in flexibly mounted gun in rear cockpit
(V-156B1 Chesapeake Mk I) Four wing-mounted 0.30in machine-guns and one similar gun flexibly mounted in rear cockpit
Bomb Load: Up to 1,500lb; could comprise three externally carried 500lb or 12 × 116lb bombs

SB2U-3

Data as for SB2U-1/2 except:
Engine: One 825hp Pratt & Whitney R-1535-02
Max Speed: 243mph at 9,500ft
Climb Rate: 1,070ft/min
Service Ceiling: 23,600ft
Range: 1,120 miles
Weight: 5,634lb (empty)
9,421 (max take-off)
Armament: One fixed forward-firing 0.50in machine-gun and one flexibly mounted 0.50in gun in rear cockpit

Above: The 'Zero' in a gentle bank to the right, providing a good view of the aircraft's upper surfaces.

Below: Low and fast, the Zero 'beats-up' the field at Okegawa.

ZERO!

Photographs by KONAN ASE

The Mitsubishi A6M *Zero-Sen* (Imperial Japanese Navy Type 'O' carrier fighter) was the most famous Japanese combat aircraft produced during WW2. This Far East equivalent of the Spitfire and Messerschmitt Bf109 acquired a legendary reputation and, like the British and German fighters it enjoyed a lengthy production run spanning numerous different versions.

In fact, over 10,500 examples of the 'Zero', or *Zeke* as it was code-named by the Allies, were built between 1939-1945, and this production total serves to underline just how significant is the aircraft pictured on these pages, for it is no less than the sole authentic, airworthy example of the renowned Japanese fighter remaining anywhere in the world.

The 'Zero' seen here is an example of the A6M5 Model 52, a variant introduced in 1943 to counter the threat posed to Japanese airpower by the Grumman F6F Hellcat. The Model 52 replaced the earlier A6M3 Model 32, and eventually accounted for over half the aggregate production of 'Zero' fighters.

'Zero' 61-120 was captured on Saipan by US forces and shipped to America for evaluation. It was later acquired by Mr Edward T. Malony, owner of the 'Planes of Fame' Museum at Chino, California. In 1978, the aircraft made a return visit to Japan where it is seen here at Okegawa during one of the numerous air displays which marked its tour.

This page: Three views of the 'Zero' landing and taxying at Okegawa. The wide track of the fully retractable undercarriage is seen to advantage. The tailwheel has no fairing doors, unlike the mainwheels, but does retract into the tail cone.

Right: During its visit to Japan, the 'Zero's' paint scheme was changed from a dark green/sky grey camouflage to an overall dark green finish on the upper surfaces and light grey undersides — a scheme which was more typical of that used during the later stages of the war in the Pacific.

61-120

N914SP

'Bear in the Air'

ROBERT E. KLING

Above: A road block training exercise conducted by the Georgia Highway Patrol, with the suspects' car in the centre of the road and one of the Air Wing's Bell 47G helicopters seen at left.

Facing page: The Highway Patrol's DHC Beaver, N914SP, at Charlie Brown airport, Atlanta, Georgia.
/ All photos with this article are by the Author

You might be driving down an interstate highway or maybe a back country road trying to make good time to wherever you are going, and then you hear those not-too-familiar words on your citizen's band radio warning of 'Bear in the Air'. The word 'Bear' in Georgia means an honest-to-goodness Georgia Highway Patrol Officer, and 'in the air' means — you've guessed it — in a fixed wing aircraft or a helicopter. Most of the time, this warning will come from a motorist who mistakes a pilot, using the road for a map, for a 'Bear' in the air. State Patrol aircraft usually do not get close enough to be spotted, at least not by the average driver of the family car or an '18-wheeler' (tractor trailer). The aircraft stay up 2,500-3,000ft and usually are off to one side of the road. The 'Bear in the Air' will have clocked you by timing your vehicle between the white quarter-mile markers on the road and then running the results through a computer. Helicopter and fixed wing pilots almost never book the actual cases; they keep the motorist in view until a ground unit summoned by Police Band radio arrives to take over.

Although the aircraft and men of the Georgia Highway Patrol's Aviation Unit do assist the 'Smokies' (ground patrolmen) and their 'picture takers' (radar) in enforcing traffic laws, they spend most of their time in emergency work such as searches for robbery suspects, escaped convicts, lost persons and even murder victims. But let's start at the beginning, when this flying unit was only an idea . . . the type of idea that would cost money, time and mean a lot of personal sacrifice.

Before it all started in Georgia, Wilson W. Weaver, the architect of what was to follow, enrolled in a flying school under the GI Bill in 1946 after serving in the US Navy during World War II. Three years later, he joined the Georgia State Patrol and, through his continued interest in aviation and assessment of its potential use by the Patrol, it was later in 1973 (and then as Lieut Weaver), that he convinced the Department of Public Safety of the need for an air branch. State Safety Director Herman Cofer gave the go-ahead to the programme in 1974 — and Lieut Weaver is now Capt Weaver, the Commanding Officer of the Georgia State Patrol's air arm.

The State Patrol's air operation began in May 1973, the first aircraft being a military surplus T-41A which had not been used for almost a year. Although officially formed in May 1974, two pilots were employed to start operations in the previous year when the T-41A aircraft was assigned to Americus, Ga. Trooper Mike Ferris, now Sergeant, and Trooper W. A. Maxwell, who is no longer with the unit, were the first fixed wing crew to fly for the Georgia State Patrol. The initial helicopter type acquired by the Patrol was a Helio Bell 47G-3B1 obtained from Davis Monthan Air Force Base, Tucson, Ariz; this aircraft was

Above right: The initial fixed wing aircraft received by the Highway Patrol for its first-line operations were the three Maule M-5s, dubbed 'Lunar Rockets'.

Right: Another fixed-wing STOL type operated by the Highway Patrol is the U-10A Helio Courier.

Below: Moving further afield in a subsequent purchasing programme, the Highway Patrol obtained three PA-18C Super Cubs from the Italian Army.

Bottom: A Bear in the Air takes an unusually close look at traffic on an Inter-State highway outside Atlanta.

delivered in March 1974. Trooper Mike Ferris flew both the fixed wing aircraft and the helicopter while Trooper Maxwell flew only the fixed wing aircraft.

The Aviation Unit of the Georgia State Patrol was officially formed in May 1974 with Lieut Wilson Weaver as the first supervisor (and qualified in the fixed wing aircraft), and with Corporal Mike Ferris as the first official pilot. The unit was located in the Georgia State Transportation Hangar at Charlie Brown Airport, though at that time the Bell 47G was still at Americus, Ga. being made airworthy by the South Georgia Technical and Vocational School under the supervision of Frank Gossett, who was in charge of the airframes and powerplants shop. Both Corporal Ferris and Frank Gossett attended the Bell Aircraft Company Pilot/Mechanic Seminar at Ft Worth, Tex, prior to full-time operation of the helicopter. The next pilot was Corporal W. A. Maxwell, who was accepted in June 1974, and, at the same time, the first Bell 47G-3B1 was put into flight operations. In July 1974, Corporal John Lane was added to the unit: he, along with Corporal Ferris, was a rotary wing-certified pilot prior to joining the Aviation Unit. By September the Aviation Unit had received a grand total of five Bell 47G helicopters.

During late 1974 pilot training was in full operation for both the fixed wing and rotary wing aircraft. Training was accomplished with the aid of military instructor pilots from US Army Forces Command

Flight Detachment assigned to the Army Aviation unit based at Charlie Brown Airport, and most of the US Army instructors worked during their off-duty hours to support the training requirements of the Georgia State Patrol Aviation Unit. Up to the end of 1974, Atlanta was the designated headquarters of the Georgia State Patrol Aviation Unit with out-stations maintained at Thompson and Tifton, and using the Bell 47Gs. The Aviation Unit's duties consisted of special purpose missions such as criminal search, rescue, surveillance and location of stolen goods.

In 1975, the attention which had been given to securing the necessary aircrew personnel was augmented to cover maintenance activities, and in June of that year the unit's first mechanic was hired.

No fixed wing aircraft for the unit's first-line operations proper were received until January 1976, but then the Law Enforcement Assistance Association allocated funds for the purchase of three Maule type aircraft. One Maule was received in January 1976 and two others in February 1976. During the latter month the unit also took delivery of one DHC-2 Mk 1, U-6 Beaver. This aircraft, with a range of 780 miles and powered by a 450hp P&W R-985 piston engine giving a top speed of 140mph, came from the Army National Guard Unit stationed at Dobbins Air Force Base, Marietta, Ga. The Beaver is used for all types of work except traffic control.

The next fixed wing aircraft, received in October 1976 from the US Army, was the civilian H-395 U-10A Helio Courier. The short take-off and landing (STOL) Helio Courier is able to get airborne after a run of only 114yd, lands in 70yd and remains controllable at speeds down to 30mph! The introduction of the fixed wing aircraft into the Aviation Unit's inventory in 1976 brought about a significant improvement in capability of the State Patrol's air arm and during the nine months between April-December the unit's operations resulted in just under 1,000 arrests and included 65 search missions. Those arrested included motorists charged with traffic violations, escaped criminals, armed robbers and other serious offenders.

The aviation division of the Department of Public Safety recorded a further expansion as well as improved performance during 1977. In February that year, three PA-18C Super Cubs were obtained from the Italian Air Force — the aircraft had once been part of the military assistance program (MAP) and were originally supplied to Italy in 1954-55.

At the present time, the unit's fleet consists of 13 Bell 47Gs (though as many as six of these are used only as sources of spare parts); three Maule M-5s; one Beaver; one Helio Courier; and three PA-18C Super Cubs. In performance terms, the unit's operating flexibility is greatly enhanced by the use of these fixed wing STOL and helicopter types; most of the former can take-off in less than 200ft, land within the same short distance, and are capable of flying over the very useful speed range of 35-160mph. The aircraft are now stationed at five points in the state. Besides the headquarters at Charlie Brown Airport, other units are maintained at Canton, Thomson, Reidsville and Cordele. This makes it possible to place an aircraft over an emergency anywhere in the state within 25min. The Aviation Unit is staffed by a total of 12 personnel who are assigned with state-wide responsibilities.

The Air Patrol gets little publicity because its primary purpose is to assist law enforcement officers at the federal, state, and local level — it does its job and then fades out of the picture. There are exceptions, of course. A call came in from the Sheriff of Haralson Country one day giving information that he had arrested several persons in a truck loaded down with marijuana. The Sheriff said that there were indications that the 'pot' could have come in by plane. Corporal Mike Chumley and Capt Weaver were assigned the task to go and check the report, and while subsequently flying over Polk County, Capt Weaver saw something interesting below. It looked like a chicken house at first glance, but after asking Corporal Chumly to turn around and take a look, both men could not believe their eyes. There was a DC-4 on the ground with no evidence of a landing strip for an aircraft of that size. This discovery was the start of the much publicised story concerning the 'The Polk County Pot Plane' later flown out from its unique hiding place and into 'stardom' to become the subject of a motion picture!

At a more mundane level, the routine operations of the unit tend to result in an average total of 30 flight hr/month per pilot with the patrol notching-up an aggregate total of some 200 flight hr/month. During the first eight months of 1977, they assisted in making 736 arrests and conducted 43 air searches in addition to putting in 64hr of road patrols. Supporting the local drive to combat narcotics traffic, they located 36 fields of growing marijuana in 1977, a single pilot finding as many as seven fields in a day while on routine patrol in northwest Georgia.

After much hard work and training, the Aviation Unit of the State Patrol is today making a valuable contribution to law enforcement in Georgia and offering a worthwhile boost to the capability of their earthbound colleagues. The 'Bears' in the air are a valuable overhead support to the law abiding motorist, and a fast moving extension of the Highway Patrol's ability to deal promptly with any emergencies. Much has been accomplished in the first five years' operations and all the indications are that a successful foundation has been built for the future.

Above: A business-like presence outside George AFB, California is that of this Lockheed F-104C Starfighter, s/n 56-0934, carrying the GA code and Tactical Air Command shield on the fin. */ Patrick J. Little*

Left: This F-86E Sabre, s/n 51-13036, sits atop a smart plinth at Bitburg AB, West Germany, home of the USAF's 36th Tactical Fighter Wing whose badge is seen below the Sabre's cockpit. */ John A. MacDonald*

Right: A Spitfire IX guards the gate of the Belgian Air Force's Technical School at St Trond. */ Archives G. Botquin*

Guarding the Gate

On poles, pillars, plinths and props of countless different designs, or sometimes parked on a prepared pavement, and even occasionally just 'put out to grass' — quite literally, it seems that no self-respecting military air base can be without an aircraft acting as gate guardian, or better still, two gate guardians — one for each side! Not just at airfields in the UK, but at similar installations all round the world, the notion of putting something impressive on the gate has long been established practice. Some of the pleasing results, which have happily extended the range of preserved aircraft on public display at bases in Europe and further afield, are seen on these pages.

Above: This Bell UH-1B 'Huey' is displayed by the 24th Aviation Battalion at Fort Stewart/Hunter Army Air Field, Savannah, Georgia. In February 1976, the helicopter was painted red, white and blue to mark the US Bicentennial.
/ Frederick A. Johnsen.

Left: Alongside the gate at Edwards AFB, California, is an example of the first US jet fighter, the Bell P-59 Airacomet.
/ J. P. Clifton

Below left: Out to grass at St Dizier air base in France is this Republic F-84F Thunderstreak.
/ Archives G. Bolquin

Top right: The Royal New Zealand Air Force acquired 48 Grumman TBF-1 Avengers between 1943-44, and the last two airworthy examples of the type — NZ2504 seen here, was one of them — continued flying until May 1959; this Avenger is now the only remaining one in RNZAF hands, and it guards the gate at Te Rapa, Auckland. */ Peter Clifton*

Right: Anchored in a final climbing turn outside Tours air base, France is this Mystere IVA.
/ Archives G. Botquin

42
NZ2504

314-TG
22

FLT LT TONY FAIRBAIRN RAF

On 24 January 1978 Argosy XR143 of No 115 Squadron took off from RAF Brize Norton to calibrate airfield aids at RAF Cottesmore during what was to be the last operational flight by an Argosy. When the task was completed and '143' returned to its Oxfordshire base, another aircraft type had flown into RAF history and another story had come to an end. In a career spanning 16 years it served safely and dependably in a variety of roles before the vagaries of defence thinking severely curtailed its use. When the Argosy retired from the transport role in 1971 the majority of the fleet was mothballed, and after plans to convert a number of aircraft to navigation trainers fell victim at the last minute to RAF contractions, the type lingered on for a further six years in the calibration role.

The military Argosy (AW660) was originally conceived under Operational Requirement 323, but the various designs submitted by Armstrong Whitworth did not result in any orders from the Ministry of Aviation. As a result the company decided to revise the design for the civil market under a private venture and the outcome of this was the civil Argosy (AW650), the prototype of which first flew in January 1959 with E. G. Franklin at the controls. Following successful trials with the civil Argosy the Air Ministry ordered 56 Argosies for RAF Transport Command and the first of these, XN814, flew in March 1961. The military role brought many changes in the basic civilian design, notably the clamshell rear doors which could be opened in flight for airdrop operations, a strengthened freight floor and changes to fuel tankage. Inevitably the modifications increased the weight of the aircraft and because of this the wing structure was reinforced and more powerful engines (Rolls-Royce Dart 101s) were installed.

First deliveries were made to the RAF in November 1961 when XN821 arrived at RAF Benson for the Argosy Conversion Unit which had been established for crew training. During the initial build-up of the Argosy force the conversion training included a

Annals of

manufacturer's course at Coventry where crews stayed at an excellent guest house known universally as 'Ma Haggis's'. The first squadron to be equipped with the new aircraft was No 114 which reformed at Benson in October 1961 and which received its first Argosy (via the Argosy Conversion Unit) in February 1962. The Argosy's official entry into service with the squadron was marked by an Open Day at Benson in March 1962 at which the Mayor of Wallingford unveiled the Borough crest on the nose of one of No 114's aircraft.

Transport Command had in the Argosy its first turbo-prop, pressurised, medium-range tactical transport aircraft and on entering service it supplemented the Hastings and Beverley force until those ageing piston-engined aircraft were phased out of service. Thereafter it remained as the RAF's principal aircraft in the role until the build-up of the Hercules force was completed. Apart from a few problems caused by the bad weather of the winter of 1962/63 the entry of the aircraft into service proceeded smoothly as evinced by No 114 Squadron's success in winning the Lord Trophy for 1962. In February of that year No 105 Squadron reformed at Benson, and deployed to Aden in the summer as the first overseas Argosy squadron. The second and last of the UK transport squadrons, No 267, reformed at Benson in November 1962, followed by No 215 Squadron which, after reforming at the Oxfordshire base, began moving out to Singapore a month later.

After the successful deployment of the overseas squadrons the Benson Argosy Wing, comprising Nos 114 and 267 Squadrons, became the mainstay of Air Support Command and No 38 Group transport

This picture: Argosy C1, XR107, of No 215 Squadron at Changi, Singapore, seen flying over the Straits of Johore in 1964. / *Fairburn collection*

the Argosy

operations, and the two squadrons carried Service units on operations and exercises to many parts of the world. NATO exercises took aircraft to North Norway, Germany and the Mediterranean, while route training flights were made to such exotic places as the Caribbean, West Africa, the Azores and Ascension Island. In 1963 the Argosy Conversion Unit moved to RAF Thorney Island to become part of No 242 OCU which then carried out all Argosy crew training. The last full Argosy course passed out of the OCU in December 1968 and thereafter crew training was carried out at the Air Training Squadron at Benson until mid-1970.

One of the most important operations flown by the Benson Wing was that to support the deployment of the Javelin-equipped No 29 Squadron, together with a quantity of radar equipment, to Ndola, Zambia, in 1965 following the Rhodesian unilateral declaration of independence (UDI). This task involved a lengthy route via Istres, Malta, Akrotiri, Tehran, Bahrain, Masirah, Aden and Nairobi. The following year the squadrons dropped fodder and supplies to farms isolated by blizzards in the UK!

Training in the transport support role continued through the medium of frequent exercises and it was during one such exercise in Libya that the Benson Wing experienced its one and only fatality. This accident involved the loss of XR133 of No 267 Squadron which crashed at the forward airstrip of Lot El Afraq in May 1968 killing all 11 people on board.

On a happier note, 1968 also saw the establishment in February of the Argosy detachment (Ardet) at Muharraq consisting of aircrews from both Nos 114 and 267 Squadrons and groundcrew from Benson's Engineering Wing. The detachment provided vital supply links between Muharraq, Sharjah, Masirah and Salalah and it was found that the Argosy was ideally suited to the route stage lengths in the Gulf. Very useful payloads could be carried on airdrop and air landed missions in support of ground forces operating in the desert. The aircraft used on the detachment became well known for the winged triple 'A' which appeared on their fins and which stood for 'Associated Argosy Airways'. In June 1970 Ardet flew the Sultan of Oman from Salalah to Bahrain for onward movement to London after he had been shot in an attempted coup. The detachment gained a deservedly excellent reputation for its work and was particularly appreciated by people serving in the remote outposts of the Gulf.

Whilst frequent exercises took the Argosy to overseas destinations, more pressing commitments kept the aircraft occupied in the UK. As a result of serious rioting in Belfast and Londonderry in August 1969 the Northern Ireland government requested military aid and the General Officer Commanding (GOC) asked for immediate substantial reinforcements. Between 15 and 27 August, 154 transport sorties (33 of them by Argosies) were flown to Aldergrove from bases in England. The following year there was more rioting during the Easter weekend and the GOC again requested reinforcements. In June-July 1970 the airlifts to Ulster reached a peak and Argosies, together with Hercules and Britannias, airlifted over 3,000 troops, 759,000lb of freight, Landrovers, Ferret Scout Cars, water cannons and armoured vests into the troubled province.

The versatility required of both aircraft and crews was well illustrated by a task in support of a Meteorological Office investigation into frontal

Left: Argosies at RAF Benson in January 1966, nearest the camera is 851 of No 114 Squadron.
/ Author's photo

Right: An Argosy of the ARDET at Muharraq takes-off along a gravel-type strip during a training sortie. */ RAF official, via the Author*

Below: Argosy C1, XP443 of No 114 Squadron dropping Italian paratroops over Sardinia during Exercise 'Follicle' in 1970.
/ MoD, via the Author

Above: The RAF's Free-fall Parachute Display Team, 'The Falcons', jumping from an Argosy. / *MoD, via the Author*

weather systems approaching the UK. For this task an Argosy flew ahead of a surface warm front at a height of 17,000ft while the loadmasters released radar reflecting sondes at frequent intervals. During the sorties the rear doors were opened and closed repeatedly and the loadmasters were exposed to temperatures as low as –25°C.

As well as No 267 Squadron's last year of operation, 1970 also saw important 38 Group exercises in widely differing parts of the world. The first of these, Exercise Thread, was mounted from Malta and involved a stream assault landing on Sicily. The exercise also featured the annual Lord Trophy which was won, appropriately, by No 267 Squadron. Exercise Arctic Express, on the other hand, was held in North Norway and was designed to test the rapid deployment and employment of NATO's Allied Command Europe (ACE) Mobile Force under winter conditions. The RAF's Air Support Command provided the UK air component, which included Argosies, for the exercise, and troops were flown from the UK to Bardufoss and Andoya. No 38 Group finished its exercises for the year with a detachment to Pisa, Italy, for Exercise Follicle which included three Argosies from Benson. The aircraft practised single drop operations, formation drops, and tactical take-offs and landings from semi-prepared strips near Rome.

The Argosy became a familiar sight to the public because of its use for several years as the support aircraft for the RAF parachute display team, 'The Falcons'. But not so well known is the fact that the Argosy was modified for possible use as a bomber in internal security operations. Several crews were even given appropriate training although in the event the aircraft was never used in this offensive role.

A complete departure from the transport role for the Argosy came with the introduction of the aircraft to calibration work in RAF Signals Command. With the designation Argosy E1, it entered service with No 115 Squadron at RAF Watton in February 1968. In April 1969 the squadron moved to Cottesmore where, alongside the Canberras of No 98 Squadron, it formed part of the Flight Checking Force. The Argosies normally performed the low-level aspects of the work which involved checking Instrument Landing Systems (ILS), Precision Approach Radars (PAR) and airfield surveillance radars. For this work the aircraft had special equipment which enabled the crew to assess the performance of the airfield aids very accurately. In addition TACAN (Tactical Air Navigation) beacons and direction finding equipment could be checked. When checking an ILS installation, for example, skilful flying and concentration over long periods were required to bring the 40-ton Argosy exactly on the glide path at a precise speed.

The majority of the Flight Checking sorties were flown in the UK but tasks known as 'Safaris' were flown to check equipment at RAF bases overseas. The first Safari to the Far East left Watton in July 1968 for Changi, Singapore, where the aircraft took up station and checked equipment at Far East Air Force (FEAF) bases. Crews were rotated by VC10 the following month. From then until the last FEAF Safari in October 1971 it was the policy to maintain a No 115 Squadron Argosy east of Suez.

Arguably the best remembered Safari flown by the squadron was that to the Seychelles in January 1972. This task, with its picturesque setting in the Indian Ocean, involved checking the VOR (VHF Omni-Range) equipment after its installation at the Islands' international airport. It was the sort of trip to gladden a recruiting officer's heart and cause the Treasury a fit of apoplexy!

In addition to calibration work, No 115's Argosies took over certain other responsibilities. These included the 'Iris' task, in January 1969, of monitoring radio conversation, which up until that date had been carried out by Hastings WJ338 *Iris III*; and the Argosy crew training commitment which had previously been met at Benson.

In February 1976 No 115 was on the move again, this time to its new base at Brize Norton where the squadron was to operate the Argosy for a further two years. At the end of that time, when the last Argosy had been disposed of, No 115 had been operating the type for 10 years, almost to the day.

The story of the Argosy's service in the Middle East began in June 1962 when No 105 Squadron moved out to Khormaksar, Aden, with five aircraft; after settling in to its new base, training and route proving flights began in preparation for the unit's new duties. Intensive tropical trials were carried out using Argosies XN847 and XN849 flying routes to Bahrain and Nairobi. At the conclusion of the trials the aircraft returned to Benson for servicing while the engines were examined by Rolls-Royce. Meanwhile the squadron's other aircraft had been flying route-

Below: A change of role for the Argosy as, redesignated the E1, it was assigned to calibration tasks with No 115 Squadron; the unit's XR140 is seen here at RAF Finningley for the Silver Jubilee Review of the RAF in July 1977. / *MAP*

proving trips to airfields on the Arabian coast such as Masirah, Sharjah and Salalah.

By October 1962 the squadron had 10 aircraft on strength and was well established in scheduled route flying in the Middle East. In addition to the route trips, No 105 also had a tactical role to perform and accordingly a tactical training programme was begun. This involved low flying and supply dropping, much of which was carried out at Sheik Othman, a disused airfield near Khormaksar. The training was extended later to include paratroop dropping. The airdrop training proved its worth when the squadron began supply dropping to troops fighting in the Radfan in July 1964. The dropping zones (DZs) in this mountainous area north of Aden were hot and high with few escape routes in the event of an engine failure.

In the same year that operations in the Radfan caught the headlines, the squadron suffered its only serious aircraft accident although fortunately there were no injuries. The dictionary defines 'Argosy' as 'a large merchant vessel' and in March XP413 underwent a dramatic reversion to type when it ditched in Aden harbour at the end of a training sortie. After a thorough drying out at Bitteswell, its birthplace, XP413 was airborne again in 1966, but a Plimsoll line later painted on the Argosy's side, about level with the pilot's knees, was just too good to resist!

At the end of the year the Rhodesian UDI led to a number of special flights, beginning with a task to fly radio transmitting equipment to Francistown in Bechuanaland. In December an intensive and protracted airlift was mounted to supply fuel to Zambia, with aircraft unloading at Ndola and Lusaka and then flying across the Congolese border to Elizabethville and to refuel for the return flight to Nairobi. During this operation a congratulatory signal was received from the Secretary of State for Defence praising the squadron for is hard work and efficiency.

As the plans for the British withdrawal from Aden were accelerated so some of the squadron's operational commitments reduced, although the moves and relocation of units resulted in an increased demand for airlift. It was planned that No 105 itself would redeploy to Muharraq and by August 1967 the move had been completed. For the last five months of its existence No 105's claim to fame as the RAF's largest operational squadron was accompanied by a proportional increase in workload before final disbandment early in 1968.

Historically the Far East Air Force has always seemed to lag behind the other RAF commands in the context of re-equipment and, although it was not the last command to receive the Argosy, the arrival of No 215 Squadron provided a powerful shot in the arm to the diverse though rather ageing transport forces operating from bases mainly on Singapore island. No 215 deployed from Benson during June-July 1963 and arrived at Changi at a particularly crucial time

Left: A No 105 Squadron Argosy C1 sits in the baking heat of the Gulf coast at Sharjah. / *MAP*

Right: A Far East Air Force Argosy C1, XP447 of No 215 Squadron from Changi, Singapore flying along the south coast of Malaya in 1964. / *Fairbairn Collection*

Below: No 215 Squadron's Argosy C1, XP445, seen during a supply drop in Borneo in 1965. / *via Flt Lt Dom Parkinson RAF*

just before Indonesia began its policy of confrontation towards Malaysia.

Officially a state of war did not exist between the two nations but during the three years of confrontation fighting did take place in Borneo, and an effective support system was essential to the type of jungle operations that were carried out. The Argosy, with its medium range and air drop payload of eight one-ton containers, proved to be ideal for this vital role.

However, the climate and terrain of East Malaysia combined to make supply dropping a demanding occupation. The DZs, usually small, were invariably in difficult flying country while tropical storms produced towering cumulus clouds and torrential rain. The mornings in Borneo began with mist in the valleys which lifted slowly. The first sortie of the day was therefore difficult because the DZ, and the high ground surrounding it, might well be obscured and there was no question of attempting to let down without being able to see the terrain. Once the mist had dispersed there was a period of reasonably stable conditions, but after midday the cumulus clouds began to develop and extreme turbulence made accurate flying very difficult. The increase in the air temperature reduced the performance of the Argosy's engines making the climb out from the DZ a nail-biting experience. It was always a relief to get rid of the first couple of one-ton containers because the Argosy was then lighter and more responsive, and hence safety

margins were that much wider. Occasionally Argosies would combine with the larger capacity Beverleys of No 34 Squadron for air dropping bulkier equipment. For instance, on one occasion a bulldozer was needed to carve out a new airstrip in Borneo. The Argosy dropped the bulldozer's blade and other smaller parts while the Beverley dropped the main body of the vehicle.

The workload of a typical crew on detachment to Labuan, a small island off Borneo, in June 1965 with XR107 illustrates the intensity of the supply dropping when the Confrontation campaign was at its peak: 7 June — $3\frac{1}{2}$hr flight from Changi to position at Labuan; morning 8 June — carry out DZ recce; 8-18 June two trips per day, every day, dropping one-ton loads to ground forces in Borneo.

Although the operations in Borneo kept No 215's head down in Malaysia the squadron also found time for scheduled route flights to Hong Kong (staging through Saigon), to Bangkok in Thailand and to Seoul in South Korea in support of the British garrison. Occasional 'trainers' reached as far as Australia and exchange visits were made with the Americans at Naha and Tachikawa in Japan where No 215 crews were able to fly the C-130 Hercules — a taste of things to come.

The author has vivid memories of flying as an ATC cadet on a low-level, cross-country training trip in a No 215 Squadron Argosy in April 1964. Climbing into XP444 the flight deck was like a Turkish bath and continued to be so as we taxied across the airfield and queued up for take-off behind a No 48 Squadron Hastings. Lifting off from Changi the temperature became more bearable as we climbed out over the Straits of Johore and began our triangular flight at 250ft over the southern tip of Malaya. As far as the eye could see there was rolling green jungle broken only by brown snaking rivers and the occasional corrugated iron hut glinting in the sunshine. Out over the east coast of Malaya we caught a fleeting glimpse of startled upturned Chinese faces as XP444 passed over a rather sinister black junk and then we were heading back down to Singapore island, Changi, and an ice cold can of Tiger beer.

However, the Argosy's days in the land of Tiger beer were numbered; the Indonesian confrontation ended in 1966 and No 48 Squadron's re-equipment with the more versatile Hercules was imminent. In October 1967, the same month that No 48 received its first Hercules, No 215 relinquished its first Argosy and the rundown of the unit was under way. The squadron was officially disbanded in February of the following

Above: Supplies tumbling away from an Argosy's rear loading ramp during a practice drop over Cyprus in 1970.
/ RAF Official, via the Author

Above left: Argosies of No 70 Squadron at Akrotiri, Cyprus in 1970. The nearest aircraft is the VIP transport, XP444 *Helios*, while others in the picture include XP449, 446, and 410; and XN847 and 821.
/ RAF Official, via the Author

year but happily No 215 Squadron's loss was No 70 Squadron's gain for several crews and aircraft went directly from Changi to re-equip No 70 which at that point was operating Hastings at Akrotiri, Cyprus.

No 70 Squadron, the last of the overseas Argosy units, had a long and distinguished career in the Near and Middle East and up until 1967 had been flying the Hastings for 11 years. After re-equipment with the turbo-prop aircraft the squadron's commitments included the logistic supply of British military and government units in the Mediterranean, Persian Gulf and Africa, Search and Rescue work and tactical supply operations. In the latter role the Argosy with its particularly suitable rear doors greatly enhanced No 70's air-drop capability and allowed a much wider variety of equipment to be dropped to ground forces than had been possible with the Hastings.

Typical scheduled flights included those to El Adem (bringing back tour-expired Servicemen to Akrotiri to catch the 'Moonrocket' VC10 to the UK); Malta — twice weekly; and Ankara. Occasionally the squadron visited Cairo, Istanbul, and Crete in support of CENTO exercises.

Tehran, with its mind-boggling contrasts of 20th century sophistication and almost medieval poverty, was always a fascinating port of call. On arrival at the airport, crews were met by an enigmatic and unforgettable character named Manny Shyster who drove up to the aircraft in a battered yellow VW. Manny, an Iranian who took care of such administrative details as passports and health documents, was all powerful and a courteous approach when dealing with him invariably smoothed the way for swiftly cleared paperwork and punctual transport. After arrival formalities had been completed the crew would be whisked through hair-raising traffic to overnight accommodation at the Elizabeth Hotel, an establishment noted for its excellent cooking, and also its locally produced vodka which most people avoided. Because of the 'hot and high' conditions at Tehran there was usually extra careful scrutiny of aircraft weights and payload before take-off from the airport for the return flight to Akrotiri the following morning.

Elsewhere in the Middle East No 70 was called upon to perform tasks that even required a temporary change of markings for its aircraft. After civil war broke out in Jordan in September 1970 the Jordanian government appealed to a number of western countries for urgent medical aid. The UK swiftly mounted Operation Shoveller in which medical units and supplies were airlifted to Cyprus. The plan was then for the medical aid to be lifted to Jordan, but technical arguments against the use of military crews delayed the delivery of the aid. The arguments over crew status were finally resolved by applying International Red Cross markings over the national insignia of the No 70 Squadron Argosies which took part in the airlift and the crews themselves wore civilian clothes for the trips to Amman.

By late 1970 the ubiquitous Hercules was beginning to filter into No 70 Squadron's inventory, but while the new aircraft was soon to form the unit's main equipment three Argosies were retained at Akrotiri until 1975 for communications duties. This mixture of types led to contemporary cartoons in the station magazine depicting No 70 (Argules) Squadron.

It was during this period that No 70 flew one of its most ironic mercy missions. In July 1974 the Cyprus National Guard staged a coup and Nicos Sampson, a former EOKA gunman, was declared president. Archibishop Makarios fled to Britain and it was a No 70 Squadron Argosy which took him to safety. The irony of the situation lay in the fact that back in March 1956 it had been No 70 Squadron Hastings that had flown the Archbishop to deportation in the Seychelle Islands; the wheel had turned full circle. The Argosy used to fly the Cypriot patriarch was XP444, an ex-215 Squadron aircraft which had been fitted out for the VIP role after joining No 70 Squadron and which was subsequently flown by a special VIP crew.

As part of Britain's withdrawal from Cyprus, No 70 Squadron moved to RAF Lyneham in February 1975 and during the same month two of the remaining three Argosies, XP412 and XP450, were flown back to No 5 MU at RAF Kemble. 'Treble Four' remained behind at Akrotiri in the VIP role, although no longer part of No 70 Squadron, until being flown home to RAF Cosford and retirement the following November. With the return of XP444 there were no longer any Argosies based outside the UK.

The rundown of the Argosy transport force in the UK began with the disbandment of No 267 Squadron

Right: A No 70 Squadron Argosy C1, XP445, at Sharjah. */ MAP*

Below: A camouflaged Argosy, XR106, of No 114 Squadron taxys-in during Exercise 'Libration', a 38 Group Force Training Exercise at Hal Far, Malta, in February 1971. */ MoD, via the Author*

in June 1970. Its aircrew joined an enlarged No 114 Squadron which also provided crews for the Persian Gulf detachment on a rotational basis. With the disbandment of No 114 Squadron at Benson in October 1971 and the withdrawal from the Gulf, Argosy operations in RAF Air Support Command came to an end. For a while it looked as though the Argosy might be reprieved when plans were made to convert a number of aircraft to navigational trainers to replace the Varsities at RAF Finningley. A start was even made on the project and XP442 was converted to T2 standard at Bitteswell in 1974. A second aircraft, XP411, was converted to a T2 by the RAF and delivered to Finningley in October 1974, but then the whole idea was abandoned and the T2 became redundant almost overnight.

The last of No 115 Squadron's aircraft, XR140, was flown to RAF Halton on 10 February 1978 but appropriately it was No 114 Squadron which first and last flew the aircraft in the role for which it had been designed. Though whether operating in the transport or the flight checking role, the 'Whistling Wheelbarrow's' distinctive shape and sound at locations all over the world, and the reliable service which it gave, will long be remembered both by those who flew it and those who simply admired it.

The development of

ALAN WRIGHT

This picture: A typical scene at a regional UK airport in May 1968, in this case the location is Abbotsinch, Glasgow in 1967. The One-Eleven has been seen on the domestic routes since British United and British Eagle joined the Anglo-Scottish operations. G-ATPL later went to Dan-Air, its present owner. The Viscount in the background was British Midland's G-ASED. / *All photos with this article by the Author, unless otherwise credited*

air services in the UK

Travel within the UK is very much taken for granted these days, yet even in the 18th century only the brave, foolhardy or those with suicidal tendencies ventured far from home. The advent of the railways changed all that. With remarkable speed and often with little thought, track was laid to link cities, towns and villages. The British public began to move.

Road transport became more of a practical proposition in the 1920s, although the railway companies did not regard it as a serious rival. A new competitor in the early 1930s did however awake some interest in the complacent minds of the soot and steam brigade. Regular air services were being introduced, pioneered very often by coach operators who were otherwise finding it difficult to remain in business.

The first private company to introduce its own airline was Hillman, a bus and coach operator in north-east London. In April 1932 the first service was flown between Romford and Clacton using a Puss Moth. It was a very small beginning, but one which proved highly successful. In the following year Margate was added to the network, to be followed by routes to Liverpool, Belfast and Glasgow by December 1934. The airline prospered, aided no doubt by its low-level fare structure which was aimed to attract passengers to the new DH84 Dragons. Operations were centred on Stapleford in Essex, where only basic amenities were offered the traveller in order to cut costs. Eventually rationalisation of routes was necessary to ensure the survival of the internal services. Hillman therefore merged with United Airways and Spartan Airlines in 1935, resulting in the formation of British Airways which in turn became a part of BOAC in 1939.

Many other airlines were formed during the period leading up to the war, but comparatively few remained active for long. The south coast resorts provided the bread and butter for Portsmouth, Southsea and Isle of Wight Aviation from the start of the airline's services in mid-1932. Flights from the island initially connected to the mainland at Portsmouth, but an extension to London (Heston) was added later. Shoreham and Bournemouth joined the network in 1934 and, until the enforced cessation in 1939, services continued with great success.

All this activity had not gone unnoticed by the railway companies who decided to create their own airline. Known as Railway Air Services, the first route plied by the new carrier was from Plymouth to Liverpool via Teignmouth, Cardiff and Birmingham in May 1934. Bristol and Southampton were connected to the Isle of Wight later that year, while a main trunk route was introduced from London to Glasgow via intermediate cities. Although now part of the airline scene, the railways did not put a great deal of effort into their airborne activities. Enough was done to obstruct the genuine private carrier, but it was, after all, not in their best interest to attract too many customers away from the trains.

They need not have worried. Despite the existence of the prewar domestic air services, the idea of using them was unthinkable to the ordinary citizen. It was something for the adventurous and those with money. There was indeed some sense in their viewpoint since the airliners of the day were not lavishly appointed, resulting in rather a test of stamina over long sectors. Then the war came, which introduced flying to thousands. Those fortunate to survive ensured the successful expansion of the aircraft industry as a whole, of which the UK air services were an important part.

Airline operations during the 1939-45 period were mainly confined to maintaining the life-line to the islands around the north of Scotland and the Scillies. To do this the companies involved achieved amazing

Above: The Viking was used extensively after the war by BEA, many of the type later passing to the independents. Before serving with Eagle, G-AJPH was the Nene test-bed aircraft.

Above left: Sivewright was one of the post-war hopefuls, using Avro XIXs and later Dakotas on a few schedules. The airline ceased operations in 1951.

results considering the problems they encountered. A few Dragons and Rapides which had escaped impressment were employed, flown and maintained by a handful of personnel. By 1944 it became possible to start a Liverpool-London service once again, but still using Rapides or the larger, four-engined DH86 Express. The organisation of the commercial flying was controlled by the Associated Airways Joint Committee who remained responsible for the activities of such companies as Railway Air Services, Scottish Airways, etc, until the end of the war.

The situation in the early days of peace altered little. By this time Jersey and Guernsey were once more joined to the mainland by Rapides, but otherwise there were no major additions to the network. Railway Air Services at least tried to improve their fleet slightly by introducing the Avro XIX, essentially a civil version of the later Anson series. This type was first used by the company on 3 December 1945 when it left Croydon for Belfast. During the month it was also announced by the Government that the ban on private flying would be lifted on 1 January 1946. It was a day eagerly awaited, but although it would permit civil operators to undertake charter work, it came as a shock to the fledging airlines to learn that no scheduled services could be flown. These, the newly elected Labour Government stated, would be exclusively for the newly created British European Airways.

It transpired that it was not at all easy for BEA to effect the take-over. Shortage of crews and equipment meant that the smaller companies continued in the normal way until finally, on 1 February 1947, the Corporation was prepared to accept all the schedules. The routes offered had increased in the intervening period to include a direct London-Glasgow service using a couple of DC-3s for the purpose, both initially in their military drab green and grey livery.

This type continued in service with BEA for a good many years, although on the trunk routes the newer Vikings supplemented them on some timings. The London terminal airport also changed, with Northholt handling its first scheduled operation on 2 September 1946. By the spring of 1948, the UK domestic services were still few in number since the flag carrier was still unable to cope with any major expansion. Several of the independents were invited to apply to the appropriate authorities to take over some of the uncovered prewar routes as well as to introduce new sectors.

This opportunity was welcomed by the numerous small carriers formed after the war. Most of the founders were ex-RAF with the memory of flying still fresh and their demob money burning a hole in their standard issue civilian suits. Alas, many did not survive long enough to receive the benefit of the slight relaxation in the official policy. Needless to say for those still active, the crumbs of comfort, however thinly scattered, were very acceptable.

The routes involved were those of fairly short length such as the Isle of Wight services from Southampton, Gatwick and Bournemouth, Shoreham-Southampton and various connections to the Isle of Man from northern cities. The Bristol Channel crossing was given to Cambrian Air Services who brought the total

Right: The Herald has served the Channel Islands since the early-1960s. BIA has gradually added to its fleet, G-BBXI coming from Itavia in 1973.

Left: Morton Air Services was another company founded in 1945. The airline's name finally disappeared in 1968 when it was absorbed into British United Island Airways.

Below: The Dakota was employed on schedules immediately after the war, a role in which it has continued ever since. Cambrian operated the type in the late-1950s and '60s until the Viscount took over its duties.

Bottom: Aquila Airways Short S45 Solent 3 flying boat, G-AKNU *Sydney* seen at its moorings at Southampton on 23 September 1956. / *Peter Clifton*

number of airlines selected to be Associates of BEA to nine.

Although better than nothing, the independents soon realised that BEA had not been over generous with the route offers. Since they were seasonal operations, there was little time available to build up traffic before it was time to close down again. Worse still, since the Agreements were annually allocated, the insecurity did little to encourage the operators. Too much success could see the route part of the main network the following year!

The situation remained the same in 1949 and 1950, although a far greater number of licences were awarded. By this time the Berlin airlift was over, with the result that more companies were seeking employment. However since most of their equipment was too large for internal services, few of the newcomers applied for route approvals. One of the exceptions was the independent flying boat operator Aquila Airways. Hitherto the airline's activities had been concentrated on overseas services, particularly to Madeira. This time the company was given approval to open up a series of domestic routes. These were intended to provide a link between the south coast — at Falmouth and Southampton — and Scotland — at Glasgow and Edinburgh.

The first service was scheduled for 4 July 1950 using Southampton only, due to handling problems at the Cornish port. A proving flight was arranged a month prior to the introduction using G-AGJN, one of Aquila's ex-BOAC Hythe flying boats. The trip to the

north was made at a leisurely pace, the 25 passengers enjoying a magnificent view from the converted Sunderland as they trundled over Swindon, Oxford, Birmingham, Manchester and Galashiels before splashing down on the Forth at Leith. The first 360 miles had taken $2\frac{1}{2}$hr, whereas the connection between the two Scottish cities took but 20min for the 53 miles. It was necessary to use Greenock for the Clyde terminal as flying boat operations were impractical any further up river. Coaches were therefore arranged for the passengers to complete the journey to Glasgow.

The flight proved very satisfatory and hopes ran high. Unfortunately the early promise was not maintained. Advance bookings were very poor indeed, forcing the airline to abandon the scheme. The Scots were still using Dunoon and Rothesay for their annual seaside excursions, with holidays in Cornwall still very much in the future. The service was undoubtedly original but before its time. Today it would probably be an outstanding success.

Almost as a consolation, Aquila was given an unexpected opportunity during the next summer to operate some Jersey schedules, due to the inability of another carrier to continue. The 'boats' flew from Southampton, landing in St Aubins Bay one hour later. The seven pounds fare was identical with normal rates but in fact the journey was faster point-to-point since no road link was necessary. However flying boats did not feature in any other route approvals for the domestic services again.

Many of the problems facing the independents had begun in 1945 when the Labour Government came to power. It was not part of their policy to allow too much private enterprise. As is common practice by whichever party is in opposition, grand promises were made by the Conservatives on the subject of a better deal if they were returned at the General Election. Their opportunity came in 1951, but there was no instant change apparent to the operators. After six months a typical politician's compromise was announced which left the Corporation's existing routes untouched, but at the same time allowed the independents to apply for all new routes whether freight or passenger.

The immediate reaction was one of disappointment, but after a time the smaller airlines realised that the situation had actually improved. Applications began to reach the authorities who, after hearing any objections, issued the approval if considered feasible. Another benefit came with the introduction of longer licencing periods, giving the airlines the comfort of greater security.

The Channel Islands had been developing prior to the war, so it was natural that many of the independents sought permission to operate these more lucrative routes. Cambrian was one of the carriers in the forefront of these activities, connecting such places as Cardiff, Bristol, Haverfordwest, Liverpool and Staverton to Jersey and Guernsey. Not to be outdone, the island based Jersey Airlines was also involved in schedules to the mainland. Southampton, Exeter,

Gatwick, Bournemouth and Manchester were all timetabled by the start of the 1953 season.

Over on the eastern side of the UK, another small carrier was gradually increasing in size. East Anglian Flying Services (EAFS) had been started in the familiar manner by a demobbed airman, Sqn Ldr R. J. (Jack) Jones. It was soon established at Southend and by 1954 included Ipswich, Southend, Portsmouth, Rochester, Sandown, Shoreham and Jersey on its schedules. The going had not been easy at times, but unlike many of its contemporaries, EAFS managed to struggle through some difficult patches.

The slow growth of the small independents was really the key factor in their ability to remain in business. Their fleets generally contained ex-RAF aircraft, particularly Dominies, which on conversion became Rapides. The type could be picked up cheaply and were readily available at first. Reliability was good and passengers were quite happy to fly in the ageing biplanes. After all, even the flag carrier still used a few. Unfortunately progress could not be halted indefinitely and by the mid-1950s carriers were forced into the bigger and more expensive leagues.

Needless to say the number of airlines remaining on the scheduled service scene dwindled still further. Many a departing company blamed their failure on the lack of consistency in the route allocation procedure, making it uneconomic to re-equip with newer and larger aircraft even if traffic forecasts proved it necessary. Others became disenchanted with the aviation business in general, turning their attentions elsewhere. Fortunately some persevered, in many cases becoming involved in a succession of purchases, mergers and take-overs.

Companies such as Airwork, British Aviation Services, Skyways and Hunting had already absorbed some of their weaker brethren by 1958. In each case a considerable shareholding was held by shipping groups which accounted for their continuing healthy state. Even Cambrian and Jersey Airlines disposed of a sizeable proportion of their stock to a larger company, in this case to none other than BEA. This move certainly saved the Welsh carrier from extinction in the lean winter months of 1958/59. Among the truly independent, Eagle was making steady progress, although most of its schedules were still mainly to European destinations. Even this airline had a brief encounter with the sea when Cunard took control in 1960, a situation which lasted three years or so. East Anglian Flying Services adopted the title Channel Airways to reflect their expanding interests, but remained firmly under the control of Jack Jones.

The marriages enabled the independents to enjoy the benefits of modern equipment. For instance, Hunting-Clan was able to keep pace with BEA by ordering three Viscount 700s in 1953, the first such company to enter the turbo-prop era. A network of services radiating from Newcastle was planned, resulting in improvements at the airport to facilitate the use of the larger airliners. The operations were not particularly successful initially, but through the years the development of the north-east has brought success to later carriers. At least the plans did awaken the authorities to the need for airport expansion.

It was not always practical to develop an airfield site, which meant ultimately the loss of a scheduled service. While the early Rapides and Dakotas in the growing years took grass runways and sparsely equipped terminals in their stride, their successors did not. Usually it was just not economic to maintain a mixed fleet purely to serve these out-dated ports of call. Typical of these in the late 1960s were Ipswich, Portsmouth, Rochester, Shoreham and the Isle of Wight airfields. It is true that Portsmouth saw a renewed burst of activity in 1971 when the now defunct J. F. Airlines flew Twin Pioneers on a Jersey service, but it was not long before the carrier collapsed and the airport ceased to function as such. Shoreham

Right: Loganair Trislander G- AYXK about to depart from Inverness.

Left and below: Like the Rapide and Dakota, the Viscount has served for many years on domestic services. Viscounts are also the mainstay of the British Midland fleet.

Below centre: Scillonia was the last of many to employ the Rapide on scheduled operations.
/ Peter R. March

Bottom: The Scilly Isles helicopter service has been operational for some 15 years, one S-61N being outstationed for the purpose at Penzance.

still has a seasonal link with Jersey, but again the size of the equipment used has been reduced to match the traffic and facilities available.

To islanders, the air links with the mainland are vital. Ever since the pioneering and hair-raising exploits of the Scottish airlines in the 1930s, the inhabitants of the northern islands have appreciated their value. Once again the Rapide was the mainstay for many years, proving indispensable on the rough strips or the beach landing area on Barra. These were really social services since there was little profit in it for the airline.

Back in Glasgow, a small independent was steadily growing. Gradually Loganair developed a number of routes serving many far-flung islands off the north and west coasts, in addition to such places as Wick, Inverness and Dundee. Eventually when BEA was left with Viscounts and HS748s in Scotland, Loganair received routes unsuitable for these two types. The carrier now flies sectors of varying length, including the shortest scheduled service in the world from Westray to Papa Westray. The route is but two miles long and is timetabled to take two minutes but usually is completed in about 70sec. It can be compared with a trip along one of Heathrow's main runways!

At the other end of the UK, the Scillies had also come to depend on their air link. Started in the mid-1930s, the service continued throughout the war, the only English domestic route to remain open. The dangers of this were emphasised when Dragon G-ACPY was lost in 1941, believed shot down by an enemy aircraft. BEA carried on postwar, still using Rapides well into the 1960s.

Several carriers attempted to improve the journey to the Islands by offering services from airports blessed with better access than that at Lands End. Mayflower Air Services was virtually a one-man, one-aircraft concern, but the single Rapide G-AHLM produced some very satisfactory returns from its work out of

Plymouth and Exeter. Unfortunately a serious accident forced the premature end of the airline in 1963. There were others keen to carry on, but which failed to survive. Scillonia tried in 1965 by employing some ex-BEA Rapides, becoming in fact the last user of the type for scheduled services in Europe. After this company's demise, Westward attempted a scheme with a difference. In addition to the south-west sectors, a Plymouth-London link was introduced using an Islander, which then spent the day on a frequent Gatwick-Heathrow shuttle before returning home in the evening. At first the idea proved successful, but gradually losses mounted and the service was closed down, followed soon afterwards by the airline ceasing to trade. So by the end of 1971 the Scillies were once again dependent on BEA, while surface transport connected the two London airports for another seven years until the advent of the helicopter link in 1978.

The only other schedule to employ the helicopter was in fact that to the Scillies. BEA had adopted the Sikorsky S-61N for its route way back in 1964, using a specially built heliport some three-quarters of a mile from Penzance. The type immediately provided a considerable increase in capacity, comfort and reliability, quickly becoming very popular with regulars and visitors alike. The operations are carried out with the minimum of fuss and with few of the formalities experienced on other routes, resulting in a friendly bus-stop type service.

Brymon Airways started their schedules in 1972, gradually building up a comprehensive network radiating from Plymouth and Exeter. The Newquay-Heathrow service was later taken over from British Midland, a route which under its new operator has grown in popularity as businessmen came to appreciate its value when visiting the expanding industrial areas in Cornwall. Gatwick passengers also have their link by using either the Plymouth bound Brymon Twin Otter or Air Westward's Exeter service which the company inaugurated in the spring of 1978 using Cessna Titans.

Of all the many UK airlines, Channel Airways probably produced more ideas than any other. Many were impractical and quietly filed away, but one scheme in particular did arouse interest. This was the proposed bus-stop operation embracing 10 airports down the eastern side of the UK. Originally planned for the One-Eleven twin-jet, this quickly proved uneconomic so when the service actually started in January 1969, a mixture of Viscounts, HS748s and Herons was employed. 'The Scottish Flyer', the name by which it was promoted, soon began to run into problems. Crew scheduling was not simple when so many landings were involved, with sectors averaging only 65 miles. Handling staff were needed at intermediate points, while load factors fluctuated enormously with the trunk centre sections receiving good support but with the ends very poorly patronised. It was inevitable that with the continued losses that Channel suspended the service after 10 months.

It was a brave try and deserved greater success. Undoubtedly the airline was just too early with the idea, since with the oil boom of the 1970s it could not have failed. Indeed in 1972 Air Anglia began picking up the pieces after the collapse of Channel, gradually adding sectors to its network so that today most of the Scottish Flyer's itinerary is included in the company's timetable.

The bus-stop idea was also developed by Dan-Air, although called 'Link City' by this airline. Originally one Dakota trundled backwards and forwards between Bristol and Newcastle via intermediate airports, later giving way to a Nord 262 for a short time in 1970/71. The comprehensive services built up are now flown by HS748s, connecting Bournemouth, Bristol, Cardiff, Manchester, Birmingham, Leeds, Tees-Side, Newcastle and Glasgow. The other main

Above: Air Westward started operations in 1978 using Cessna Titans.

Above left: One of Brymon's Twin Otters taxying at Plymouth.

Below: A few members of Channel's fleet were earmarked for service on the 'Scottish Flyer' in 1969. Viscount G-AVHK was one of these and is seen wearing the appropriate legend.

Bottom: The Trident is to be found on many of British Airways' trunk routes. Originally a member of Northeast's fleet, G-AVYD was written off at Bilbao in 1975.

operators of UK schedules tend to concentrate on single sectors, although British Island Airways does include several routes involving transit stops.

The main trunk routes have always been with the flag carrier, although both British Eagle and British United helped to change the pattern in the 1960s. Their appearance on the Anglo-Scottish routes rapidly produced jet airliners in order to attract passengers. It was not really justified since the existing, almost purpose-built, Vanguards were ideal for the operations, the time saved by the replacements being insignificant. But in the interest of progress the type was prematurely retired from the routes.

Probably the most noteworthy change on the domestic scene came in 1975 when British Airways introduced a shuttle service between London and Glasgow, followed later by a similar arrangements to Edinburgh and Belfast. The idea was to offer a simple no-frills, guaranteed seat service with minimum fuss. It has become a very successful operation using Trident 3s on a two-hourly frequency with Trident 1s as back-up as necessary. However the simplicity of the scheme has been unfortunately rather lost as a result of the need for security in these troubled times. Nevertheless if the paper work and checks are accepted as a fact of life, then the advantages more than compensate.

The current UK domestic network owes much to the oil industry around the British Isles, but other businesses too have learned the benefits of speedy travel. The services available are as comprehensive as they have ever been, covering most of the areas of industry and population. Although the private citizen accepts the trunk routes in a matter-of-fact manner nowadays, it may still be some time before the public automatically consults airline timetables for short journeys. But then progress is a strange thing. Who would have thought that with bus companies removing their conductors that British Airways would introduce fare collectors on the Shuttle!

This picture: Perhaps the most famous Boeing 707 of all is this -320B bought by the US Government and equipped for service as the personal aircraft of the President of the United States. 'Air Force One', as s/n 62-6000 is known, carries the military designation VC-137C; it was in this aircraft that Lyndon B. Johnson was sworn in as US President on that fateful day in Dallas, Texas in November 1963 after the assassination of President Kennedy.
/ Boeing